BEST FOOT FORWARD

JOY JUNG

This book is a product of Smart Success, LLC.
For more information see www.BestFootForwardCareer.com

Please join our eGram series discussing job search issues @
www.BestFootForwardCareer.com/egram

DEDICATION

To Rob, my husband and my editor,
who gave selflessly of his time, support and expertise.

TABLE OF CONTENTS

Forward

APPENDICES

ACKNOWLEDGEMENTS

I would like to thank my sister, Gay, for her support and proof-reading abilities: my sister-in-law and exceptional peer, Marikay, for her professional advice and support and my friend and colleague, Bedley, for her professional council and encouragement.

FORWARD

This guide is written for the job seeker from a recruiter. It is focused on tips and techniques for candidates to implement in their job search, specifically: resumes and interviewing. The tips are from my personal experience as a corporate recruiter as well other recruiting peers who reviewed and offered suggestions. These tips and tools are intended to help guide and offer assistance in the job hunting process. As a corporate recruiter for a variety of different companies and industries, the tips and tools covered are universal.

This guide was also written for the job seeker who has experienced a job loss. Rarely is this scenario covered in most job search books. I firmly believe, from my years as a corporate recruiter interviewing these individuals, until the job seeker has dealt with the job loss in a positive and proactive manner, they will be stymied in their search and landing the next position. I urge you to read and complete the activities covered in the first part of this guide. It is truly in your best interest. Give prospective employers the opportunity to see and know you at your best.

As the job seeker, you take the lead in finding your next job. This is a daunting task. It can be a full time job, a very tough, lonely full-time job. There are no secrets, mystical formulas or magic mantras. As the candidate, you will make this process unique and special through your experiences, skills, credentials and attributes.

Knowing yourself is the key to creating the next step in your career path. Knowing yourself can be a complex issue. For our purposes, there are three major components which are essential to finding that next job that fits "just right:"

> **Know yourself – Be realistic**
> **Know yourself – Be focused**
> **Know yourself – Be a winner**

While the words are simple, the process is not. It is time-consuming, requiring a lot of soul-searching and asking others for help and support. It is time well spent because you are worth the investment.

BEST FOOT FORWARD

JOB LOSS

Job loss is near an all time high in the United States today. There is no guarantee of security within a job, a profession or even an organization. It can happen to anyone regardless of position, company, gender, age, or race. Even those who operate their own businesses can lose everything. No one is immune to losing their job. Everyone has been touched by it. For some, it has been through their family and friends, and, for others it has been personal. It has happened to you – you've lost your job.

This trend started several decades ago. In the 1980's, it was blue collar workers who became displaced or obsolete. In the 1990's, it was the white collar workers who faced a reduction in the workforce. Now in the 2000's, it is whole organizations who are facing elimination or bankruptcy. Through these years, corporations have tried desperately to improve the bottom line in order to gain a competitive edge in the marketplace. The easiest and quickest way they thought to accomplish this goal is to layoff employees.

This guide was not written to detail the reasons or the causes of our current economic situation. It was written for those who are living with the results of these conditions, those who have lost their jobs. A job loss creates a tremendous impact on one's self esteem. For most of us, our jobs help to define us, give us a purpose, provide our livelihood and support our families. When this is taken away, it is a powerful influence, not only on our lives, but, on those around us as well. The impact of a job loss has been compared to the loss of a loved one or the end of relationship. In fact, we have lost a loved one – ourselves. We so closely define who we are by what we do, that, when we lose a job we can lose ourselves if we are not careful.

Friends and family members may try to be supportive and helpful. However, unless they have also experienced the job loss cycle, they really have no idea of the phases you will be going through. They could be empathetic and caring or walking on eggs around you. They may even be afraid to bring up the situation and leave you feeling more isolated. They may even be angry putting you on the defensive.

The good news: the loss of a job, if handled carefully and responsibly, can be resolved. As you will see, the quicker you can let go of the past, accept the present, and begin to envision a new future, the quicker you'll find the new job or new career. In this situation, you take the lead. It will be your responsibility to work through this process and allow others to help and support you as well. It is a serious undertaking. It is hard work but the reward will be well worth it.

Stress and the Loss Cycle

The loss of a job, with all the emotional mayhem, physical manifestations and mental anguish, is real. Death of a loved one and loss of a job are two of the most stressful events an individual can experience. For many individuals the workplace had become their second home and family. The work gave purpose and meaning to their life as described earlier.

After we lose our job, our first thought is to find a new one. In fact, we even put more stress on ourselves by thinking this way. I believe there are a few steps we need to take *before* we start looking for that next job. Recognizing, understanding and dealing with this stress are vital before we begin the job search process.

You may be thinking to yourselves, is this author nuts or what? Please read on. I have been involved in recruiting and outplacement for several years, actually over 25 years at this point. In particular, I have worked for three major organizations in the outplacement arena and counseled thousands involved in the job loss process.

In working with individuals who are going through the job transition process, it is imperative for a job seeker to know and transition through the job loss process. The job loss process involves:

- **Stress**
    - Recognizing and handling stress
    - New stress of job loss
    - Old stress of everyday living
    - Taking action to reduce stress

- **Grief Cycle**
    - Acknowledging grief
    - Understanding of continuous cycle
    - Active transitioning

The Grief Cycle was originally introduced by Dr. Elisabeth Kübler Ross in 1969, in her book *On Death and Dying*. Dr. Ross, through her work with terminally ill patients, recognized and referred to a cycle of emotional states which has become synonymous with the Grief Cycle. This Grief Cycle has five stages: denial, anger, bargaining, depression, and acceptance. Since its' introduction, the Grief Cycle has been applied to a wider spectrum which now encompasses anyone going through a perceived negative change, such as a job loss.

With my work in outplacement, I have identified additional emotional states for individuals going through a job loss.

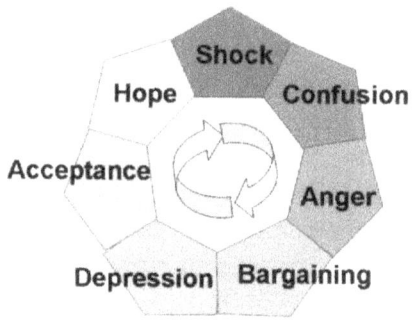

THE GRIEF OR LOSS CYCLE

The first stage is shock, even if, there have been rumors or discussions of job loss. This is followed quickly by confusion, then anger, bargaining, depression, acceptance and then hope. For the individual to be a successful job seeker, hope is the key. A job seeker with hope will accomplish great things.

For job seekers, stress is a reality. The stress of living, of meeting obligations, of providing for your family, of finding another job, etc. I've provided a more detailed discussion of stress in the next chapter. Finding a new job or a new career is stressful. How a job seeker deals with stress will determine their effectiveness in finding a new position or career. Stress and its effects are real as outlined in the next section.

THE EVER-PRESENT DAILY STRESS

Through my experience as an outplacement consultant, I have defined the Job Loss Cycle as the emotional states of job loss plus the compounding effects of stress.

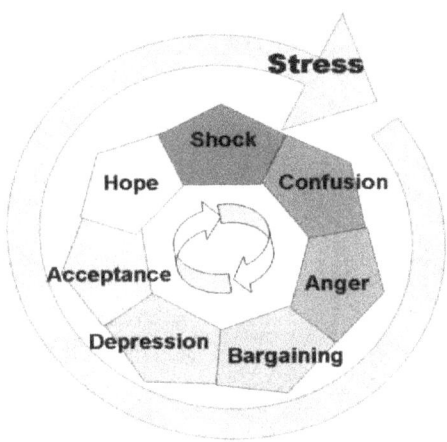

JOB LOSS CYCLE

This cycle is discussed in detail later in the Job Loss Cycle section. If you have experienced a job loss, the information discussed in Writing About Job Loss could be vital to your success in obtaining the next position.

Stress

Stress is one of the most primal instincts humans possess. Stress, in a life-threatening situation, is the classic "fight or flight" trigger. The body and mind are both involved in the response which is controlled mainly by the release of the adrenaline. The changes are quite powerful and useful:

- Adrenaline mobilizes sugars, giving the body access to more strength, energy and stamina. This helps the body to fight harder or run faster.

- It reduces the blood supply to your skin and short-term to the inessential organs. This minimizes bleeding if you are hurt and ensures energy is not wasted on processes not immediately useful.

- You may experience nausea or diarrhea: this eliminates excess weight that might otherwise slow you down.
  (A detailed description is provided in Appendix B.)

Stress involves three factors: body, mind and change. If there is any change in our body (weight change, menopause, health issue, pregnancy, etc), we become stressed. If there is a change in our mind or life (death of a loved one, job change, marriage, new child, new home, etc), we become stressed.

It doesn't matter if the change is "good" or "bad", we become stressed.

Anytime there is a change, whether it is real or a perceived change, we become stressed.

Stress has been defined as external pressure which causes internal anxiety, in another word: worry. Stress is a part of life. Many psychologists believe stress is inevitable. We have issues which provide stress everyday (drive to work, job, school, family, etc.) and issues that may only happen once in our life (loss of a mate, death of a child, major health issue, retirement, etc.)

When we are worried, we are stressed. The loss of a job is one of the most stressful situations an individual can go through. For the job seeker, this worry is about:

- Finding the next job

- How to begin looking for a job

- Putting food on the table

- Paying financial obligations

- Family issues

- Health issues

- What is the next step . . .

Knowing and understanding this stress and how it may affect the mind and body better prepares the job seeker to re-enter the job market and be an effective and successful job candidate.

There are two major types of stress: acute and chronic.

Acute Stress:

Acute stress is the most common form of stress. It comes from demands and pressures of the recent past and anticipated demands and pressures of the near future. It is short-term. It is usually associated with current life issues (what's going on now, what just happened, or what might happen tomorrow.)

Chronic Stress:

Chronic stress is "long-term" stress. This is the unrelenting stress that wears individuals away day after day, week after week, year after year. Chronic stress destroys bodies, minds and lives. Chronic stress comes when a person never sees a way out of a miserable situation. It's the stress of unrelenting demands and pressure for seemingly interminable periods of time. With no hope, the individual gives up searching for solutions. Chronic stress is usually related to pressures at work, long-term relation-ship problems, loneliness or persistent financial worries.

Unfortunately, while job seekers may recognize the symptoms of acute stress at the onset, chronic stress seemingly sneaks upon the individual. When the job seeker continues to be in a state of chronic stress, what was once abnormal becomes normal. Chronic stress becomes familiar and sometimes, almost comfortable. *For example:* take sleeping through the night. Many job seekers who are experiencing chronic stress report they do not sleep well, or for short periods, or sleep is not restful and they begin to take this as normal behavior.

Symptoms of stress are easy for job seekers to overlook or dismiss. For job seekers, the most common symptoms are:

- Emotional distress – some combination of anger or irritability, anxiety, and depression (the three stages of emotions.)

- Muscular problems including tension headache, back pain and jaw pain.

- Stomach, gut and bowel problems such as heartburn, acid stomach, flatulence, diarrhea, constipation and irritable bowel syndrome.

- Performance may be enhanced in the very short-term but will decrease over time if stress continues.

Acute stress is highly treatable and manageable. However, if not treated, or if the depression or anxieties continue to plague the job seeker, it could lead to chronic stress. Job seekers who become chronically stressed generally feel unhappy, fatigued, lethargic or irritable. They may be easily angered. Because the body is under attack for a long period of time during chronic stress, the symptoms above continue to escalate if action is not taken.

Please see your family physician for any of the above symptoms.

Everyday Chemical Stressors

In addition to the stresses of losing a job, a surprising amount of the stress the job seeker may experience on a daily basis can be caused by chemicals you consume. This is especially true for the job seeker because you may be emotionally unstable. During this time, it is hard for the job seeker to monitor their habits or take the best care.

By eating or drinking certain things, we can actually put our bodies under chemical stress. If we are eating an unbalanced diet, we are stressing our bodies by depriving them of essential nutrients. Eating too much over a long period can lead to obesity. This puts your heart and lungs under stress, overloads your organs and reduces stamina.

Habits such as smoking, drinking alcohol or caffeine may take on more significance and usage may increase. This is one way job seekers try to relieve stress, unfortunately, it does not work.

Caffeine, in coffee and chocolate, is a stimulant and actually raises levels of stress hormones. It does this by leaving the general blood stream and entering the brain. It makes it more difficult to sleep and can make you more irritable.

Chocolate usually is combined with sugar. Sugar causes the body to increase its production of insulin in the body to deal with the increased glucose in the bloodstream. This may provide more energy short-term, but using it constantly stresses your body by the fluctuating amounts of insulin that your body produces to "level" the glucose in the blood.

Alcohol, in larger amounts, increases stress because it disrupts sleep and damages body organs.

Nicotine's toxic effects raise the heart rate and puts additional stress on your body. If you smoke, try taking your pulse before and after a cigarette and think about the difference.

These websites offer valuable information on stress:

American Heart Association, www.americanheart.org

National Mental Health Association, www.nmha.org

American Institute of Stress, www.stress.org

Dealing with Stress

At this point, you, the job seeker, may be thinking, *"I knew I was stressed out before but now I am really stressed out thinking about stress."* The good news is there is hope. You, the job seeker, can change the way you function under stress.

It takes a conscious, consistent effort employing these three steps:

1. **First Step**

   Acknowledge the stress.
   Once you know what you are dealing with, a solution can be found.

2. **Second Step**

   Address the stress. Most job seekers have three choices:
   i.   Accommodate it
   ii. Alter it
   iii. Avoid it

3. **Third Step**

   Action

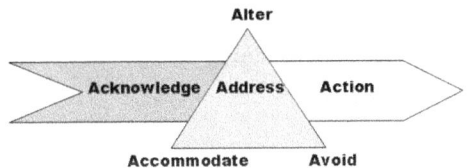

THE THREE STEPS OF DEALING WITH STRESS

Looking more closely at the three steps:

- ❧ **Acknowledge Stress** -Give it a name – what is causing the stress?

- ❧ **Address Stress**–Make decision – how to deal with above stress?
  - ❧ **Accommodate it** – Understand this stress is inevitable and find a way to cope.
  - ❧ **Alter it** – Can this stress be changed? – defer, defuse, etc.
  - ❧ **Avoid it** –Can we circumvent or take it out of the equation?

- ❧ **Action** -Create an action plan using the one of the three techniques above and follow through.

Using the method above, acknowledging the stress or defining the stress, helps the job seeker understand all the pressures, real or imagined, they have placed upon themselves. When individuals allow stress to paralyze their life, they give up. Acknowledging stress gives the job seeker concrete information to deal with. It is similar to getting a diagnosis from your doctor. Once the disease or condition is identified, knowing what medicine to give or protocol to use can be determined.

Once the stress has been identified, then there are three methods for combating the stress: accommodate it, alter it or avoid it. The first method, accommodating stress, means understanding this stress will not go away – maybe it's the stress of finances. Accommodating this stress may entail finding a part time job to help cover expenses or having a family meeting to discuss ways to reduce their monthly expenses or both or some other technique.

The second method, altering the stress, may require creativity. This could involve refinancing of a loan, moving to another city for more job opportunities, moving to a smaller home, etc. In this method, techniques are used to reconfigure the item(s) causing stress.

The third method, avoiding the stress, should be used on those items that detract and derail your job search. One example is worry. Worry is wasteful and should be avoided. It will have a de-bilitating effect. Worrying about something will not get anything accomplished. When worry pops up, confront it and take action when you can. If not, then write down the worry and give yourself permission to deal with it later.

All of the above methods may require support and help from friends and family. Do seek counsel. As stated earlier, some stress is inevitable. However, even the effects of this type of stress can be reduced. To help in this endeavor, the job seeker should address all aspects of their life: physical, mental, spiritual, and family (friends). All these areas can provide coping mechanisms to provide a holistic approach to dealing with stress. Cultivating ways to cope with stress in each of these areas will make the job seeker stronger and better able to deal with the entire upcoming job search issues.

Here are some areas to include or review for reducing stress:

- **Physical**
  - Balanced Diet
  - Exercise
  - Relaxation Techniques
  - Sleep

- **Mental**
  - Set Realistic Goals
  - Prioritize Activities
  - Positive Affirmations
  - Positive Attitude

- **Spiritual**
  - Prayer
  - Meditation
  - Worship
  - Commitment

- **Family** (community)
  - Strengthen Family Bonds
  - Volunteer
  - Stay Involved

A few tips are given on the next page for dealing with stress. Since each job seeker is unique, your answers need to come from inside you. There are a variety of books, websites, programs and organizations to help find the ones that work best. Your family physician or an employment counselor at the local state employment agency may also provide help or information.

BEST FOOT FORWARD

Tips to Cope with Stress

Relax
Each day schedule a few minutes of quiet time
(Reflection, prayer, meditation or taking a hot bath)

Exercise
Engage in 20 – 30 minutes of exercise
(walking, jogging, yoga, swimming, other)
at least three times a week

Sleep
Get plenty of sleep – at least 8 hours every day

Caffeine
Reduce caffeine by cutting back on coffee, tea, chocolate
and caffeinated sodas

Organize
Set your priorities by simplifying your life
Organize your closets
Learn to say "No"

Socialize
Spend time with family and friends
Develop a new hobby
Learn something new
Volunteer

Share
Share your feelings and thoughts with someone you trust

Eat
Have, at least, one hot meal everyday
Eat more fruits and vegetables

Laugh
Rent a comedy video
Read the cartoon strips
Get a funny day calendar
Find a humorous website
Spend time with someone who makes you laugh

Avoid
Trying to do too much.
Negative influences – TV, individuals, etc.
Medicating with over-the-counter drugs (sleeping pills, etc.)
Using alcohol to relax

The Job Loss Cycle

As most of us know who have gone through the loss of a loved one, the grief cycle is not just a one time through process. However, I can tell you from personal experience, as this cycle repeats itself and the individual works through these cycles, the emotions and tensions become easier to handle. As with a loved one, the memory will never go away but the pain and hurt do ease.

But you are probably still asking, "So what?" What does this have to do with losing a job or finding a new one? It is important, because, until the job seeker is ready to address the loss of their job with a stranger, in a stressful setting in a professional manner, such as an interview, the job loss will come back to haunt them.

The worst thing a job seeker can do is break down during an important interview because they have not dealt with the job loss, or, say something negative or stupid about their former employer. These things do happen. I have actually seen individuals go down a path during the interview that they know they shouldn't but they can't help themselves. The dam finally breaks.

> *While working at a job center, one of my roles as a job counselor was to conduct or role play "a job interview" with the clients. This one afternoon, Mike, an engineer who I have given some resume pointers to, wanted to role play an interview. He had a real interview scheduled the coming Monday and he wanted to be more prepared.*
>
> *The interview session was going well until I asked the famous question, "Why did you leave your last job?" The minute he opened his mouth, I knew he was in trouble. His shoulders slumped, his eyes were downcast as he stated, "Well, it was like I was on the Titanic. We all knew she was going down and there was nothing we could do about it." At this point, a single tear escaped and clung to his left cheek. Mike turned beet red and just looked at me.*

At this point, I called "time" for our role playing and we talked about his answer. Mike was not ready for a "real" interview. He still needed to deal with his job loss.

In this situation, Mike had not worked through his job loss. Plus, he had not thought through the interview process to have an answer for the job loss question. In a real interview, Mike would have not gone any further because his emotional state would cause questions to be raised about his professionalism and his emotional stability.

I have experienced job loss through personal family members and years of working in outplacement with a variety of professionals and industries. I have learned there are predictable responses or stages individuals go through when suffering a job loss. Let's now look at them in detail.

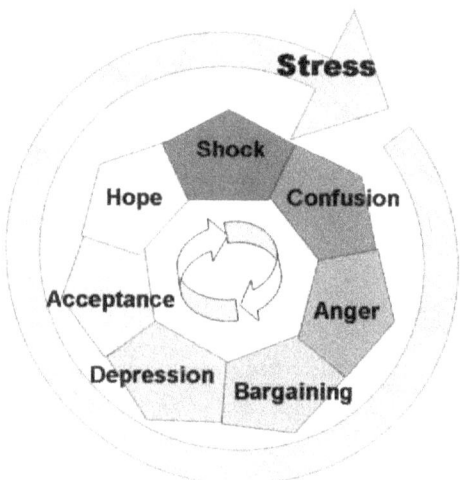

THE JOB LOSS CYCLE

BEST FOOT FORWARD

The Seven Stages of the Job Loss Cycle

1. Shock

While it is called the grief cycle and there are seven stages, individuals go through the cycle at their own pace and in their own way. The first stage is shock. Even though we may have been told that our job may be ending, until it really happens, we really don't believe it. That's when shock takes over. Shock is one way the mind has of protecting itself. The loss of a job, the pain, the distress is just so overwhelming, our mind shuts down. We do not want to think; we cannot think. This may cause some individuals to withdraw. They hear nothing, they see nothing, and they say nothing. Others may go into an automatic pilot mode, maybe if they act like nothing happened, nothing did. While others may actually feel pain, a sharp gut reaction. A few others immediately want to fight or seek a higher authority to reverse the decision. Any and all of these emotions are real. The job loss is real.

2. Confusion

Confusion and shock seem to be almost synonymous. They appear together and are often closely associated. Confusion is when the job seeker cannot focus. You may start to do a task and then completely forget what you are doing and why. For the job seeker this is compounded by the loss of the daily routine. For many of us, our job defines who we are not just what we do and this can happen without the job seeker even being aware of how affixed their self-worth and ego have become to the job. For years, our lives have revolved around our job, when to go to work, when to take vacations, business trips, even social requirements such as dinner meetings may all have been planned and arranged for us. Now this is all gone. Confusion can begin almost immediately. Some of the symptoms job seekers experience at this stage are:

- Inability to develop a routine
- Lack of concentration

- ❧ Difficulty making decisions

- ❧ Anxiety

- ❧ Lack of motivation

This will be a time of great stress. I have heard of those who did not want to get out of bed, others who couldn't remember how to make a cup of coffee, and some who ate their way through the day. Be kind to yourself. Losing a job is an emotional situation. Give yourself the opportunity to grieve for a day or two. Acknowledge the loss of the position but do not become obsessed with the loss. It was a business decision. You, and all your talents and skills, are very much alive and kicking.

The best way I have found to deal with this lack of motivation or concentration is to take small steps. Our behavior can be changed by our actions. Deliberate, small successful actions will ignite the path for more actions to follow. This is a sampling of the steps the job seeker may take to help alleviate or work through this stage:

- ❧ Develop a routine – set up office hours (See **Regular Office Hours** *section*)

- ❧ Talk to an employment counselor, pastor or other individuals who have transitioned through a career change or job loss or who help individuals through these situations.

- ❧ Start the networking process – begin with friends, relatives and others sympathetic to your situation. Give yourself some time before you begin networking, at least a week or two. Use this time period to work through the initial shock, grief, anger and other hosts of emotions you will be experiencing initially after the job loss.

- ❧ Let go of the past – start visioning a new future – create a transition plan

    ❧ Remove items from your sight or home that remind you of the past position (calendars, pens, plaques, golf shirts, etc) Box them up for now – deal with them later.

Following any or all of the suggestions above will help the job seeker define their new work of finding a job or career. As an example, setting up routine office hours may give the job seeker the impetus to get up and get dressed. You may only be able to stay focused on finding the next job for only 30 minutes or so at the beginning. As you continue to get up, get dressed and show up, you will find this time span increasing.

3. Bargaining/Guilt/Fear

Bargaining/Guilt/Fear rotate often during this stage of the job loss cycle. Fear is usually the first to emerge since it is a common component of everyday life. Typically it is broken into two types, fear of the unknown and fear of the known. For the job seeker, the fear of the unknown takes on greater significance, they are starting with a clean slate and some have no idea how to begin or where to start.

At this point, guilt may start to fester. The job seeker begins to wonder what they did wrong or what could they have done better. Some even begin to feel guilty being at home while others are still working.

Bargaining is one way job seekers try to gain control. It provides a reason for action. They think, "*If I do this, then . . . .*". Bargaining is a desperate attempt to regain control. Many job seekers want to believe bargaining can bring solutions, it doesn't. It just delays the real actions which can bring success.

Effective ways to deal with Bargaining/Guilt/Fear:

    ❧ Write down all your questions. Get them out in the open. Create an action plan to get answers.

    ❧ Acknowledge it is okay not to have all the answers. They will come.

- Recognize the finality of the job loss. Let go of the past. Don't take it personally. This is one of the most difficult processes to go through because, for many of us, our job is our identity. It is who we are, not just what we do. It is also like a death, we go into mourning. Companies are continuing to downsize or right size. It was a business decision. Determine to move forward towards a better tomorrow.

- The best way to combat guilt is to not let it take hold. When those thoughts enter your mind, immediately banish them. Learn to use positive affirmations, scriptures or quotations to redirect or focus your mind.

- Set realistic goals in other areas of your life. Recognize the importance of this special time and use it wisely.

  - **Family** – Talk to your family about the job loss, ask for their suggestions and support.

    Brian had lost his job eight months previously. He and his wife "talked" about the job loss and she was very supportive. However, at their family reunion picnic, Linda was asked repeatedly about his employment status. In pain and frustration, Linda blurted out, "Brian, what is wrong with you? Why can't you find another job?"

    They spent the next hour secluded in the family car talking about what was going on in their lives. Linda had been holding in her thoughts and feelings, trying to maintain a positive outlook for Brian and the family, while he had been keeping some of his disappointments from her as well. In the end, it literally exploded in their faces.

Develop a family night – play board games, take turns making the meal, go to a park, attend more school activities with your children, finally get to those small home improvement projects you have been putting off, etc.

ॐ **Personal** – Practice relaxation techniques, eat healthier, volunteer at a local hospital or senior center, take free on-line courses, learn a new skill, read books or listen to motivational speakers, etc.

ॐ **Financial** – Analyze budget, reduce costs, and control savings. Look for ways to reduce the monthly expenses. Ask for input from your family, get them involved. Call or talk to the local utilities and credit card companies about your current job status to determine if there are any discount programs or other discounts you may now be qualified to receive. Find other outlets instead of going to the movies or eating out.

4. Anger

For job seekers, anger is a natural emotion in this process. Anger is one way the job seeker tries to take control in a seemingly powerless situation. All job seekers experience some level of anger. It's important to recognize and deal with this anger in a safe environment and in a positive way. The symptoms of anger are:

ॐ Inability to concentrate

ॐ Increased irritability

ॐ Headaches

ॐ High blood pressure

ॐ Digestion problems

ॐ Emotional outbursts

Anger can have both positive and negative results. When anger is turned inward or toward someone else, it negatively impacts the job seeker. It can be all consuming.

When anger is used to fuel your actions to obtain your goal of a new job, it is productive. Use it to ignite your positive attitude. This is the best way to use your anger.

Make it work for you as the job seeker. As you achieve goals, give yourself rewards: a time out, an afternoon at the movies, or a picnic in the park, etc.

5. Depression

Depression, for me, is the easiest emotion to slink into (pun intended.) It's taking those few extra minutes lying in bed in the morning which may turn into not getting up before noon. Walking around the house in pj's and not wanting to see or talk to anybody. It could be an overwhelming feeling of sadness, or, of being rejected. Some job seekers can't stand the sight of food, others can't leave it alone. (They think, at least, I have control over something.) Some want to stay in bed all day while others can't seem to sleep a wink. Their ability to put a thought together or to concentrate is nil. There is a general apathy that consumes them. Their world becomes smaller and smaller.

Depression can strike during any phase of the job search. Do not underestimate the power of depression. It can undermine your career plan by:

  ❧ Causing doubts about your ability to obtain a new job

  ❧ Raising issue with sending out yet another resume

  ❧ Feelings of fatigue and hopelessness

A productive job seeker will be diligent to guard against depression. One of the easiest and least expensive measures to ward off depression is to walk. Get outside, breathe the fresh air, or, get on your treadmill and listen to a motivational speaker. Stand up straight. Keep your head up and your shoulders relaxed. Take deep breaths to oxygenate your body and your brain.

Maintain a set schedule: waking up, office hours, exercising, play time, going to bed.

Employ positive affirmations everyday.

Eat more fruits and vegetables.

Write about the job loss. This is one of the most positive methods to work through the Job Loss Cycle. It prepares the job seeker for the job hunting tasks ahead. (See *Writing about Job Loss*)

6. Acceptance

For job seekers, acceptance begins when you start to let go of your previous job. It is acknowledging the job was lost. For those who have allowed the job to define who and what they are, this can be a transforming process. You still possess the unique skills and talents utilized in your last position. The job does not define you – you define the job. Acceptance is also learning to forgive yourself and releasing the guilt. It is the realization that, it is time to move on, and, you begin looking for new opportunities. Acceptance is:

- Letting go of the past

- Living in the present

- Taking one day at a time

- Recognizing your unique skills and abilities

7. Hope

Hope follows acceptance. The human spirit thrives on hope. Without hope, I believe, all would perish. Hope, while seemingly a fragile emotion, is stronger than steel. There are several ways to build hope for the job seeker, they include:

- Living with gratitude: Each day for a month, write down three unique things for which you are grateful (No duplication during the month)

- Go walking with a good friend who is supportive and encouraging

- Get out in the sunshine

Hope gets you up in the morning.

Hope tells you to make one more phone call.

Hope encourages you to take another look at the ads.

Opportunities are available.

Now is the time to start!

Let go of the past
Accept the present
Envision a new future

Writing About Job Loss

Writing about job loss is one of the best methods for helping individuals go through a career transition process. Many outplacement firms require their clients to write about their experience during their initial participation in the coursework. This is due in part to the research conducted about job loss. One of the leading researchers, Dr. James Pennebaker, Department Chair of Psychology at University of Texas, Austin, has written extensively about the links between traumatic experiences, expressive writing and physical and mental health.

Dr. Pennebaker discovered physical health and work performance can be improved by simple writing and/or talking exercises. He published "*Writing to Heal: A Guided Journal for Recovering from Trauma and Emotional Upheaval*" to help individuals improve their performance and healing process. He suggests recording your deepest feelings and emotions about the job loss for 15 to 20 minutes a day for four consecutive days can begin the healing process. This transcribing of your experience into something black and white you can see and touch brings improvements in what psychologists call the "working memory" (ability to think about more than one thing at a time.) Individuals who have written about their job loss have seen dramatic improvements in both physical and mental health attitudes. Specifically, this has improved their attitudes during job interviews which helped decrease the time in finding employment.

Pennebaker discovered job seekers who wrote about their feelings were actually releasing their emotions rather than repressing them. This is especially true concerning the negative emotions involved in a job loss.

A national outplacement firm also conducted a study concerning the expressive writing process. One-half of their volunteers were told to write emotionally about their job loss while the other half were given an option to either write unemotionally about their job loss or concentrate on their resumes and cover letters. At the end of this study, the volunteers reported:

- More than 50% who wrote *emotionally* were now employed

- Less than 25% who wrote *unemotionally* were now employed

The biggest difference between the two groups was a positive attitude. Volunteers who had written emotionally about their situation had processed their job loss and moved on. They were energized for a new job and a new life.

The main reason the job writing exercise is so important is it allows for negative thoughts and feelings to express themselves in a safe environment and not when the recruiter ask you, *"Why did you leave your last job?"* Recruiters can sense an individual's energy. If it is positive, the job seeker is ready for the next step – a job.

Writing exercise:

For five consecutive days, schedule 15 to 20 minutes to write down your feelings about the job loss or layoff, describe how it has affected you professionally and personally:

- Record the good and the bad. (It may all be bad.)

- Write down your emotions.

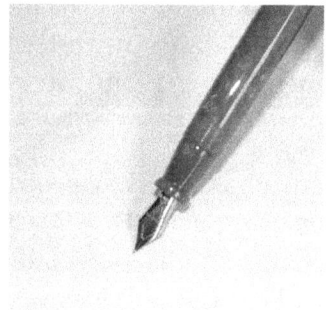

- Do not edit – just write.

- Do not think – just write.

- Do not justify – just write.

- Write. Write. Write.

You may share your writings with family or friends or counselors or you may chose to shred the papers. It is your call. (My recommendation is to shred – leave no physical evidence – leave it all in the past.) The main purpose of this activity is to write emotionally about your job loss experience so it can be put behind you.

I remember one outplacement client, Dan, an electrical engineer, who had been laid off at age 53. He had been a manager of small motor design with 12 other engineers reporting to him. At first, he was devastated, then, the anger took over. Even during the most innocuous conversations, his emotions would come through.

During the anger writing workshop, Dan was very vocal about how stupid and useless the exercise was. When I looked at his paper, there was nothing written on it. My first thought was he was not even giving the exercise a try. (For once, I kept my mouth shut and continued with the workshop.)

After the workshop was over, I talked to Dan privately about the exercise. He said he dictated most of his office correspondence. After some discussion, I suggested Dan first dictate his thoughts and feelings and then write them down from the recording.

About three weeks later, Dan walked into the outplacement center with a great big smile on his face. He came directly over to me. "I want to thank you for your writing suggestion." When I looked puzzled, he reminded me of his writer's block and the solution. "I never thought doing something so simple would actually help."

The next time I saw Dan, it was to congratulate him on his new position.

Job Loss Cycle – A Changing Continuum

The Job Loss Cycle is a continuous cycle. It is not a one-time through process and the job seeker is done. There is no set time period for the Job Loss Cycle process. There is also no set number of times the job seeker will go through the cycle.

Various elements may have less effect as time passes, such as shock and confusion. Anger or bargaining may decrease. However each time the job seeker goes through the cycle, it will seem less intense and the time spent in the acceptance and hope stages will get longer.

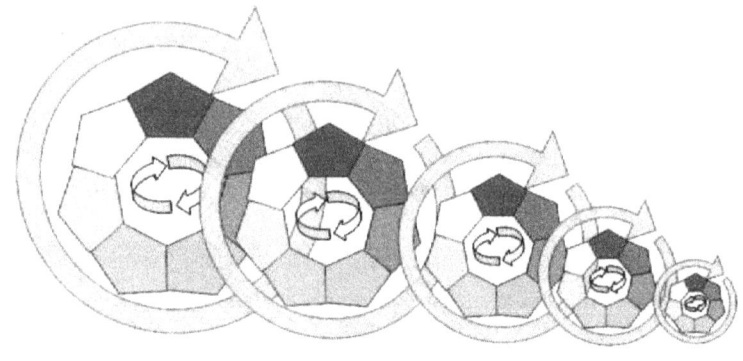

PROACTIVELY DEALING WITH JOB LOSS CAN LEAD TO A REDUCTION IN PERSONAL STRESS

Each job seeker will be affected differently and how each job seeker will react may be different. However, a job seeker who can quickly work through the first five stages and remain in the acceptance and then hope stages, are the first to find new positions.

FROM THE RECRUITER'S STANDPOINT

Job seekers understand the process from their perspective. Most of us, at one time or another, has looked for and found a job. We know it can be a long, drawn out and fairly exhausting process. However, I believe, very few of us ever take the time to appreciate what has to go on behind the scenes before the ad is placed and then use this information in our best interest. Since my job as a corporate recruiter is the counterpart to getting the next job, let's take a look at what recruiters have to do, BEFORE, the first job seeker's resumes comes across their desk. Understanding these steps will help us as job seekers to anticipate needs from the prospective employer and provide information in a timely and professional manner.

Before a job opening is announced, companies spend a considerable amount of time and effort assessing their best course of action. When a position becomes available or there is a need for an addition, the company will first evaluate the necessity for the position. This may include exploring other alternatives such as outsourcing the work, distributing the workload to other employees and even determining the validity of the position. Once the decision has been made for replacement or addition, several departments become involved to provide resources. Along with the hiring manager, human resources provide the structure and tools for the hiring process. Their duties are as follows:

Hiring Manager Create the job description and define the competencies

Human Resources work with the Hiring Manager on the above items, plus help determine position grade, salary, interview questionnaire, posts position internally and externally (newspapers, company website, major recruiting websites and other job-specific websites, third-party recruiters, local colleges/universities and job programs, etc.)

Employees are usually given a specific amount of time to express their interest and are given preference. After all, the company is already making an investment in their future. Sometimes a company will evaluate both internal and external candidates at the same time.

Companies expend a lot of resources looking for the candidate with the best **fit** for a position. Hiring the wrong person can be costly. The cost of finding and hiring the best candidate can cost as much as the first year salary considering the time and expense associated with finding, screening & interviewing candidates, training new hires, advertising and other related administrative activities. This money will be lost when a poor hiring decision is made. There is a lot at stake for recruiters, hiring managers and their companies. Hiring decisions are serious business. As a potential candidate, understanding the procedure can provide some leverage in the hiring process, streamline the job search and make the best use of personal resources.

The recruiter or human resource person is key in this process. The recruiter's main focus is to find the candidate with the best fit for the position. It is their job. They are being paid for reviewing and recommending candidates who meet the job description. It is very important from the job seeker's viewpoint to acknowledge this role. Working with the recruiter is the easiest and usually the quickest way to get to the hiring manager. A lot of time and effort can be expended if the job seeker tries to work around the recruiter.

There are two types of recruiting personnel:

    A. Company recruiters

        Work for the hiring company usually in human resources whose job function is to post job opportunities, review candidates' information and make hiring recommendations.

B. Recruiting professionals:

    a. Company contract agents – paid through an on-going contract to supply and recommend personnel.

    b. Job seeker's agent – paid by job seeker to look for opportunities.

    c. Independent agent – paid by company when their recommended candidate is hired.

In this guide, the focus will be on the company recruiter.

The job seeker's resume & application will first be seen by the recruiter. For a positive first impression, the job seeker must apply only for those positions for which they have the necessary experience. The job seeker must have at least 80% of the job requirements to be considered qualified. Remember, the recruiter must bring only qualified candidates for the hiring manager to review – that's their job. Only individuals who already have the qualifications for the position will be considered.

Recruiters do not have the *time or resources* to determine if the candidate *can or would* obtain the necessary qualifications. Typically, company recruiters are looking for candidates for a variety of positions. Many handle between five and fifty while those with major companies have 100 or more positions to fill. Please note these are all in various stages of the process leading up to the final hiring decision. So not only is the recruiter dealing with many candidates for these positions, they are also dealing with hiring managers and other recruiting support staff.

The recruiter's time is a valuable commodity. They are evaluated on the length of time it takes to fill a vacancy. A short time period equals a good evaluation. This is the main reason they consistently look for candidates who are qualified, possess the credentials and experience for these vacancies at first glance, from the resume or the application. They do not have the time or other resources to check out every candidate for every position.

It is the candidates' responsibility to inform the recruiter upfront of their viability. Recruiters who have many jobs to fill have a very limited amount of time to review candidate information. In corporate America, after reading two pages, most recruiters move on to another candidate. Many make a "go" or "no-go" decision after reviewing the resume for less than 30 seconds. Resumes should fit on one or two pages, even if you have over 25 years of experience.

Recruiter's job is to find candidate with the best fit in a timely manner.

Recruiters do not call to "fill in the blanks." They call when a job seeker has provided enough details to suggest there is a fit for the position. Calls are not made to candidates who apply for positions above their skill level. If the position is for management and the candidate does not have management experience, the resume will go in the recycling pile. From the recruiter's perspective, it is a waste of their time and of the applicants for applying.

When working with any recruiter who is helping you to find a job, remember it is a professional relationship. *Please note:* any information shared with the recruiter will probably be shared with others within the company to help describe the candidate. However, do provide any information which will help the recruiter determine your specific qualifications for the position. This may include more detail on past experiences, credentials not listed on the resume or personal career preferences such as willingness to travel.

Safeguard all personal information – only share what you want to be shared with others. Do not provide any information you would prefer to remain confidential. This professional relationship applies to all recruiting personnel.

Put a positive spin on your preferences or experiences, such as:

Usually Say: *"I don't like to travel."*

Best Stated: *"I would be willing to travel 10% to 20% of the time."*

As a job seeker, maintaining a positive attitude is imperative throughout this process. A positive attitude conveys confidence and a can do optimism.

Candidate Fit

Once a recruiter has determined a candidate has the qualifications for the position, many will then evaluate if the candidate is a good *fit* for their company. Rarely have I seen this issue addressed in a job seeker's guide. **Fit** deals with the candidate's *personal preferences and motivations* in relationship to the specific job and to the corporate culture of the organization. **Fit** is how well the job seeker's personal preferences and motivations mirror the needs or demands of the position and emulates their culture.

 One way to grasp the concept is to compare "fit" in job hunting to "fit" when looking for a new suit. There may be 20 black suits hanging on the rack. After careful deliberation, the individual selects three suits to try on. They may all look good on them, however, two of them seem right, but one may be perfect or "fits" just right. It looks good. It feels good. It "fits".

I went to the University of Kentucky so basketball is a part of my life. At the end of the 2008-2009 season, Billy Gillispie, the UK basketball coach, was let go after two years of a seven year contract. At the news conference announcing his release, the Athletic Director, Mitch Barnhart said: "He's a good basketball coach. Sometimes it's not the right fit."

Fit can be an elusive measure. The candidate may be able to do the job. They may have the technical skills, abilities, and the behaviors for the position but do they *want* to do the job? Is there a good match between the candidate and the position? Is there synergy between the candidate and the corporate culture?

One of the biggest causes of job dissatisfaction and turnover is not matching the candidate to the position. In the example above, Billy Gillispie defined his coaching job as recruiting great players and coaching them – Period. He did not believe he should be an ambassador for UK as well. His boss defined the job as both the coach and an ambassador. In the end, it was not a good match and the employee left. It should be noted the interview and the decision to hire Gillispie was made within the first twenty-four hours of their initial meeting. This may help to explain why most companies take some time in the hiring process. They want to ensure a good hiring decision is being made.

Fit cannot be listed or defined on a resume. A candidate might be able to do the job, but something makes it dissatisfying and, there-fore, de-motivating or there is part of the job that the candidate does not embrace. Candidates who dislike certain responsibilities and activities required for job success might either avoid them or perform them unsatisfactorily. Having a good match will increase the likelihood the candidate will not only take the position if of-fered but they will like the job, stay in the position, and perform successfully.

Fit is a measure of the personal satisfaction the candidate will have in the position or find the work personally satisfying. Employers are looking for candidates who have a good *fit* for the position.
*(Note: **Fit From The Candidate's Perspective** and **Character Circles** section.)*

KNOW YOURSELF – BE REALISTIC

The first step in searching for a new career is to understand what it is you like to do, what skills & abilities you possess, what characteristic traits you have, and, where your areas of expertise can be utilized. Any architect or builder will confirm a solid foundation is crucial for a building's stability and longevity. As a candidate, knowing your capabilities is your foundation along with any degrees, credentials, and certificates you have attained. Your career will be built based on these just as a building is constructed on a foundation.

Knowing your specific talents will provide confidence and poise when looking for your next position. Determining your areas of interest or expertise will also help focus your job search to those employers who need your particular skills. Companies are looking for individuals who are focused and competent. Individuals who use a scattergun approach are seen as inept and desperate by corporate recruiters. They avoid these types of resumes and individuals. Recruiters can sense when a candidate is desperate and once that scent has been noted, the candidate is history.

Worksheets have been provided in the appendix for those individuals who have not formerly completed this type of information or to act as a guide to help in the job search. Several of these worksheets help in defining areas of expertise and interest more clearly. These worksheets are tools for the savvy candidate to implement to their advantage.

There are a variety of methods, books, detailed lists, tests, assessments and other tools to assist you in this process. Universities and public libraries are good sources for information on career choices. The World Wide Web is another viable resource for information on careers as well as assessment tools, personality testing and company information. There are also other ways of looking for a career option such as talking to individuals who have "neat" jobs or recognizing a need for a service or product and filling that need.

If you have been laid off and your company is providing outplacement services, take advantage of this opportunity. Go to the workshops with a receptive and inquiring mind. Glean as much as you can from the instructor and others who have gone through this process before.

Whether you have been laid off or just looking for a better position, a good source for tools and testing is your local state job center. Many provide tests for free as well as list current opportunities. The job centers have career associates who assist in the job search process. Look for additional community resources in your area, such as your local technical or community college. Many of these provide tuition help and other support if training is required.

BEST FOOT FORWARD

Career Strategies

There are a variety of ways to look for a job. In today's market, a job seeker may need to use several different strategies when looking for a new career. All are valid and some can be used in conjunction with each other. The job search strategies being used today in the 21st century are:

1. **Find a job – any job**

    This strategy may be the one most candidates start with first. It is a successful strategy when used with poise and confidence. It can be used by someone who likes to work, needs the structure of work or wants to pay the bills. This strategy, when done properly, will take a lot of effort. It requires that the candidate think about each position and what they can bring to that position. The resume should be tweaked for each position as well.

    The candidate needs to be careful when using this strategy not to come across as *needy*. It could signal someone who is desperate - wants a job, *any* job. (The scent of "desperation" is a negative when looking for a job. A recruiter can sense it over the phone or smell it during an interview. Once the scent has been received, a job offer will not be given.)

2. **Work as a temp until something good comes along**

    This strategy is being used today by both candidates and employers. Temporary jobs are used in most industries and in a multitude of positions. It is a lot more than just administrative support.

    Many companies hire only through temporary agencies or have jobs that are only filled by the use of temps. Working as a temp allows both the worker and the company to determine if there is a "fit" between them.

Temporary jobs are short-term and have a definitive beginning and end. Finding a reputable temp agency to work
with as a partner in this process is a definite plus. Interview
the temporary agency as a prospective employer. These are
some questions to ask:

- How many positions in your area of expertise they
  have filled?

- Number of employers they represent?

- Average length of temporary positions?

- How many conversions (temp to hire) made in previous six months, etc.?

The temp agency can become your best press agent or a
brick wall in finding your next position. Once you are working as a temp, maintain contact with the temp agency – and
not just for your paycheck either. Provide *positive* feedback
about your assignment and co-workers, detailing tasks un-
dertaken and completed. This helps the temp agency understand your particular skills and abilities so they may better utilize your expertise for future positions.

3. Explore other avenues of employment

This strategy broadens the employment market for a candidate's skill set. This is an opportunity to explore other options, other avenues of employment and fulfillment. If you
have worked in the private sector, this is an opportunity to
explore non-profit, government (local, state or federal) or
public service. Other avenues could be trade associations,
teaching or other public service organizations.

The federal government is definitely expanding in the
21st century. It employs over 2.7 million workers and is
the largest employer in the United States, providing work

for about two percent of the nation's work force. Federal government jobs can be found in every state and large metropolitan area plus internationally in more than 200 countries. The website for government opportunities is www. usajobs.opm.gov. It is a comprehensive site listing all federal opportunities. Taking the Civil Service Examination will also help facilitate this process and provide information on what jobs may be available based upon your ranking.

Other valuable resources offered by the federal government are located on-line at the Bureau of Labor Statistics (www. bls.gov) under "Resources for" then select "Jobseekers." Information includes hiring outlook for many occupations, typical salaries, overview of industries and jobs along with a host of other valuable insights and websites. The BLS's two handbooks, *Occupational Outlook Handbook* and *Career Guide to Industries* are excellent resource tools for any jobseeker. Another helpful government website is: www.doleta.gov/jobseekers/career_options.cfm at the Department of Labor.

The local state employment center is one of the best resources for career information.

4. **Volunteer – charities, professional organizations, schools, libraries, etc.**

Use this time to volunteer. It keeps the mind and body active. Volunteers are needed in all organizations and come from all walks of life. Candidate may use their knowledge or skills to improve or upgrade organizational services, provide cost-effective solutions for the organization and may also acquire new skills. Staying positive and focused during your transition is crucial and giving to others provides a positive outlet as well as a sense of accomplishment.

5. Go for the dream job

Discovering your dream job can be a long cathartic process causing you to look deep into yourself to find what really excites you. Investing in a career that brings enjoyment & fulfillment and not just a paycheck is a dream for most job seekers. As in any search you have to be realistic about how you match up with your desires. Use this time to research your specific interests and career opportunities. This strategy may take more time and other resources if your goal requires building new skills and credentials. Gaining these additional skills can make you a more attractive candidate to prospective employers. Several intermediate steps and jobs may need to be taken to get to the ultimate dream job.

6. Go for the dream company

You've always wanted to work for a specific company. Find out all you can about the company. Make contact with several people who work there by joining trade groups or organizations that employees from your dream company belong. Be flexible about the positions available. If you are working for a large company, it is easier to move once you are in the company than trying for your ideal job as an outsider.

7. Start your own business

This is one of the hardest strategies to implement. Be on guard against scams. SCORE, www.score.org, is a good resource and sounding board. SCORE is a nonprofit association dedicated to educating entrepreneurs and is a resource partner with the U. S. Small Business Administration.

Another resource for reviewing potential scams is www. ripoffreport.com for online business opportunities.

Remember in starting a new business you must approach it the same as if you were looking for a job in a company. You must be focused on what you want and realistic about your capabilities. Most small business fail because the owner only understands the business activity, not the nuts and bolts of accounting, human resources, sales promotion and, yes, even basic management. You may need to get additional education to broaden your skill set or be prepared to pay for these professional services.

This is not an all inclusive list. It is an example of what individuals are doing in this job market. It is important to have and implement a strategy.

The job seeker may spend an average of 20 to 30 hours a week involved in the job search in some way. Time is a very precious commodity. The smart job seeker will use their time wisely. One of the best ways to use time wisely is to have a focused or targeted job search strategy.

When you fail to plan – then plan to fail.

Regular Office Hours

If you currently do not have a full-time job, looking for the next job becomes your full-time job.

A job provides our lives with meaning. It gives us objectives. We have things to do and usually a short time to get them accomplished. Our jobs give us a reason to wake up in the morning. Approach this transition period from a "job" standpoint. Set up regular office hours. This time will be specifically dedicated to looking for a job, reviewing opportunities, improving job skills, etc.

In any endeavor, the top two reasons why people fail are:

1. Lack of motivation
2. Lack of skills (Training, Knowledge)

Job seekers are especially prone to failing based upon the first item above. That's why it is so important during this transition time to maintain a consistent schedule. Continue to get up at a specific time. Maintain or develop an exercise program. Both the mind and the body need to be engaged.

Looking for a job can be a lonely existence. If you have skills that can be used by a community or non-profit organization, then volunteer an hour or two as mentioned previously. This is also a good opportunity to meet new people and explore other options.

Create a daily schedule, including times to:

- Make calls

- Conduct research

- Send out resumes

- Apply for jobs
- Informational meetings

Create daily, weekly or even monthly goals to help you obtain the next job.

Stay Involved

Remember:

- Respond to requests in a timely basis

- Keep notes
  - Phone calls
  - Resumes sent
  - Individuals contacted
  - Interviews

- Set up realistic, definable goals
  - Daily
  - Weekly
  - Monthly

- Mark successes
  - Place colorful stickers on calendar (different stickers for different goals)
  - Favorite cup of cappuccino with a friend
  - Something that works for you (treat yourself)
    - walk in the park
    - reading a book
    - woodworking
    - crafts
    - _____
    - _____

KNOW YOURSELF – BE FOCUSED

Recruiters are looking for candidates who are focused in their job search. A focused candidate is one who has an understanding of their abilities, the skills to successfully implement them and seeking employment in their area of expertise. Recruiters are looking for focused candidates because they exude confidence. Once contact has been made, it is the candidate's responsibility to convince the recruiter they have found the best fit for their open position.

Todd was interviewing for a communication specialist position and he had done his homework. He walked confidently into the interview room with a small valise in his left arm and extended his right arm for a firm handshake.

He had reviewed our company's profile and other information on our website. He carried copies of announcements, company campaigns, employee programs he had been involved with as well as worksheets detailing budget projections and final implementation costs. He also had prepared questions concerning our advertising partners and practices.

What a delight it was to interview him and the conversation seemed to flow easily. It was evident Todd had prepared for our interview and was focused in this career objective.

Result: He was hired.

Having a focused, consistent objective will help the job seeker maintain a clear, concise message. This message is conveyed both verbally and non-verbally. Non-verbal messages such as lack of company research, ambivalent attitude and awkwardness affect the interviewers negatively.

Recruiters are looking for competent, focused achievers. They can and do read the verbal and non-verbal messages. Come prepared for the interview. Candidates should also keep an open mind when they meet the interviewer. This enables the job seeker to showcase their background and capabilities in the best possible light.

Job Research

Job research is a continuous process of seeking and investigating opportunities. Narrowing your job search to areas of specific interest will help define and focus your search while effectively utilizing the time and effort applied.

Research can be conducted at home, public libraries and places you may choose to meet someone for an informational meeting. There are several ways to conduct this research as given in the list below.

Methods of research:

    A. Research on specific company or industry

        1. Company Websites

        2. Annual Reports

        3. Newspapers (Delivered to your door, On-line)

        4. Magazines (Business, Professional, Hobby, On-line)

        5. Family members

        6. Friends or acquaintances who work at the company

        7. Professional associations, volunteer activities

        8. Books written about CEO and other company officials

    B. Informational interview

        1. Someone who works/worked there

        2. Someone whose job you admire

    C. Tailor research for specific job

        1. Determine specific skill sets required

        2. Determine specific training needs

        3. Highlight current skill sets

Read as much as you can about a company before you plan to meet with someone who works there. Being knowledgeable about the discussion topic is top priority for any job seeker.

There are several different groups or direct formats the job seeker can use in their search. Some of them may overlap. The most common groups are:

- People You Know
- Industrial Directories
- Employment Agencies and Search Firms
- College Career Center

People You Know

There are several sources for this group based upon your social interactions. These individuals could come from:

- Family
- Friends
- Professional associations (Rotary, ASME,
- Civic associations (Scouts, PTA, etc)
- Church/Synagogue
- Christmas card list
- Club memberships
- Former suppliers/vendors/customers
- Former bosses/employers
- _____

Contacting this group is best done in a friendly and professional tone. Use your "Elevator Speech" (described and created in

Appendix K), asking for help for job leads or referrals. The job seeker may follow up with a resume for their review which provides additional information about qualifications and credentials along with job expectations.

As an example of the personal touch, set up a lunch or coffee time with someone who has an interesting job, interview them, ask them how they got started, what particular skills are needed, etc. Asking someone to talk about their particular job, industry or interest is less threatening than asking them for a job or if they know of any available opportunities. During the meeting you can discuss your desires and strengths as a way of sharing information. Please review the section on "Informational Networking" for more details.

Industrial Directories

The availability of professional contact information has greatly increased in the digital age. These directories can be used to gain information about a company, their scope of business, locations, company executives and other pertinent data. At one time, the best source of these directories was the local library, now most of these groups are on-line:

- Moody's Industrials
- Dun & Bradstreet
- Poor's Register of Directories & Executives
- Harris Directory
- Thomas Register
- Trade magazines

Employment Agencies and Search Firms

Employment agencies, search firms and your local state employment agency are three groups who assist in your job search.

My personal advice – be leery of fees and stay away from firms who want to collect a fee from you. There may be times when fees are necessary, such as testing or asking for transcripts, etc.

College Career Centers

Universities and colleges have a college career center for their new graduates and, in many cases; they also have an alumni placement office as well. This is one of the best sources for opportunities since their personnel interact frequently with employers. At the very least, they could provide contact information for a variety of employers. Even if you are located in another city, it would be worth a phone call to explore how their services may assist you.

Direct Formats

Direct formats are the venues actively seeking job applicants, such as:

- Internet
    - Global recruiting websites (Monster, Yahoo Jobs, etc.)
    - Specific company's employment page
    - Professional or Association website job listings
- Want Ads
    - On-line
    - Trade journals
    - Specific newspapers (Library or on-line)
        - Wall Street Journal
        - New York Times Sunday Edition
        - Chicago Tribune
        - Los Angeles Times
        - Local newspaper
        - Newspaper where you are looking to relocate

A resume and cover letter are usually the basic items required when submitting your information. In some cases, salary information may also be required.

For most company websites, an on-line application is also completed as part of the applicant process.

While searching for a job may be a lonely and frustrating experience at times, it is also filled with many opportunities to connect to those around you. Learn to seek and take advantage of those connections.

BEST FOOT FORWARD

Performance Posture

When looking for the next job or career move, exemplify the **4 P's**:

- ❧ Positive Attitude

- ❧ Perseverance

- ❧ Patience

- ❧ Professional

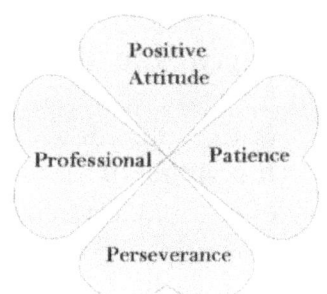

Positive Attitude

It sometimes seems like everywhere we turn, someone is telling us to have a positive attitude. There are so many things it can affect in our lives from our physical health to our mental health to spiritual health. I am also going to tell you a positive attitude is critical during the job search process as well. Most notably because of the way it can affect your job search presence! Looking for a job is a stressful situation. A positive attitude will help ease this stress and guard against the negative thoughts and influences job hunting can induce. Please see the section on ***Poise and Confidence*** for more information on a positive attitude and creating positive affirmations.

Perseverance

Perseverance is remaining constant to a purpose, idea or task regardless of obstacles or difficulties. Whether you are looking for a job while you are currently employed or you are in a career transition, perseverance will help you stay the course. It is very easy to get distracted or become discouraged in this process. Maintaining a consistent schedule and tackling a "To Do" list are two ways of building perseverance. It is not about how you feel. It is about accomplishment. You have a goal or purpose of finding a new job. Perseverance will keep you on track.

Patience

Patience is the ability to stay calm, serene and focused. Our emotions play a big part in our daily life. During a job search, it is so easy to be flying high one day from a positive phone interview to plunging to the deepest depths from a rejection letter the next. Safeguarding our emotions is indispensable to our emotional well being as well as our physical well building. It is vital that job seekers safeguard their emotions. Becoming emotional, especially during an interview, is seen as immature and unprofessional. Increasing patience will give a broader perspective of the job search process and not allow for focusing on one incident.

Professional

Treating others with dignity and respect creates a positive, professional working environment. Job seekers should maintain this demeanor whether at home or at the office. By doing so, the job seeker reinforces their psyche which in turn provides motivation for continuing the search. I have know individuals who have lost their job that get up every morning and still put on a tie because it keeps them in the correct mind set. Learn what works for you. Maintaining a professional image is vital, from how the phone is answered, to dealing with the cashier at the supermarket.

There is only **one** chance to create a positive, professional **first** impression.

> *Ryan was one of the most professional individuals I have ever met. He was always dressed in a suit and looked like he could walk into a boardroom at a moments notice. This helped to set Ryan apart from the others that I counseled in the career transition center a few years ago. Most of them wore jeans or other casual attire. The only time I usually saw clients in a suit was when they had an interview scheduled. I'll admit, my curiosity got the better of me and one day I asked Ryan, "Why did he always wear a suit?" He stated, "I want to be prepared.*

You never know when you may meet someone at lunch or going for coffee." He also showed me his business cards that he had prepared to hand out for these impromptu meetings.

While the suit may have been an outward manifestation of professionalism, Ryan also actively demonstrated this attribute through his conduct and caring of others. He was always ready to lend a hand or an ear.

Along with the suit, Ryan always wore a smile on his face. During one of the many workshops conducted at the center, another client, Tom, showed signs of depression, stating, "He would never find another job as good as the one he just had. He was too old to start over again." Ryan countered by saying, "As long as you feel that way, then you'll never find a better job. Hey, what about Bob, did you hear about his new job?" (Bob had indeed found a better job with more pay and he had a similar background to Tom.) Ryan always seemed to find a way to get a positive outlook.

Ryan also kept a notebook or journal of the contacts he had made, recording action items and other notations. He had a plan and he worked it. He worked smart and hard.

Good news – he got a great job!

Career Networking

Networking is one of the oldest and most successful methods used in employment searches. It is best employed when the job seeker has a focused career strategy. Career networking is asking individuals to help in your career search. It is a two-way street. The most successful networker will always be utilizing their network both for their benefit and to benefit others. It is a way of sharing and helping others. If there is anyone who you have helped in the past, now is the time to let them know of your current situation.

Each person has what psychologists call a concentric circle of influence or a base of friends, family, and acquaintances. Individuals within your own family will know others that you do not know. Think about what happens when you throw a stone into a lake. The stone hits the water and a circle or wave is formed surrounding the place where the stone went in, then another wave is formed outside of the first wave and so on and so on. By asking others to ask their friends, you are tapping into their base. This will allow you to reach out to their circle of friends as well. The best way to start is with someone who you have helped in the past.

While your ultimate goal is a new job, your first call is to inform them of your career search, providing them with information about your career interest. This information is known as the "Elevator Speech." It is a short, usually 30 seconds or less, summary describing your background: work experience, employers, special skills, education or training and career interests. It is used to generate interest in your skills and abilities and demonstrate your effectiveness as a communicator. It is a must in every job seeker's campaign. Memorizing it is a must. This summary can be used as a short introduction, provide a synopsis of your work experience, or showcase special skills and abilities. *Please see Appendix K for creating yours.*

During your conversation, ask them to call if they hear of something or if they would be willing to review your resume. Never put the person on the spot or demand they help. Remember this is a give and take process. Following up with a short email or note is recommended, *a thank you note is always appreciated,* it may even set you apart from others who have called in the past.

Names of individuals can be obtained through the following networks:

A. Asking friends and family who they know either in specific professions or companies, etc.

B. Asking other members of any professional, civic, church or synagogue, volunteer or other community groups (to which you belong) for names of contacts

C. Calling the company and asking for the name of the person who heads the department where your skills and experience would be best utilized, such as: Accounting, IT, HR, Sales, etc.

D. College graduates – many colleges and universities have a career center for alumni and have personal relationships with many company recruiters.

Informational Networking

This technique is used to meet with individuals at their work site or a neutral setting. It provides the job seeker with more information either about a career choice or an employer choice. It is an opportunity to continue in-depth research. This interview is for information only. It is not about asking for a job.

Once you have a specific name, send them a resume with a short letter stating that you will be contacting them in the next day or two for an informational meeting. Asking for an informational meeting is one way of not putting pressure on the individual to have a job opening or even to know of a job opening. However, it does show you are interested in the company and want to know more about their products and services or you have interest in their chosen career – such as engineering, accounting, network computing, graphic design, etc. Call the individual and ask for an appointment. If someone else answers the call and ask why you are calling, say: "They are expecting my call." If voice mail answers, leave a message stating you will be calling back. Call at least twice a week. Give them an opportunity to return your call.

Once you have the person on the phone, use your "Elevator Speech" as a way of introduction to express your interest in their career path or company.

Before your appointment, conduct research into the company – never walk into any type of interview or meeting without some knowledge of what the company does, how long it has been in business, who its customers are, etc. Prepare a list of questions as well. This could involve asking about current trends in the industry, the individual's career path or what specific skill sets they possess to be successful in their job, etc.

At the conclusion of the informational interview, thank them for their time, state politely and succinctly your interest in their company and provide follow–up information such as a resume or business card for their use. Ask them if it would be okay for you to contact them again. If they say "No", then do not contact them.

Send a "Thank You" letter within five days after the informational interview with the statement that you will be contacting them again if they gave you permission to do so. If not, please leave it out but still send the "Thank You" letter. (See *Thank You Letters* in this guide)

Many companies only accept candidates through their websites. However, the savvy job seeker will make a personal contact within the company. (As an employee incentive, many companies offer a "hiring bonus" to employees if they recommend a candidate who is hired for a position.)

KNOW YOURSELF – BE A WINNER

Winning is an attitude. Winning is anticipating. A winner has a positive attitude and is prepared. A winner in the job market effectively utilizes these two tools:

1. **Resumes**
2. **Interviews**

This guide is written for the business professional; therefore, the resume section will focus on resumes for the business world. Interviewing is more of a universal concept but once again this guide will focus on the most common types of interview questions and two interview concepts utilized in corporate America.

Resumes

A resume is the "introduction" tool for job seekers. Resumes help recruiters decipher or sort through candidate information in a structured format. They provide information about the job seeker.

Resumes are objective and subjective at the same time. They are objective because it lists information about an individual's career, such as companies they have worked for, job titles, employment dates, etc. Resumes are subjective because they detail attributes the writer wishes to highlight to prospective employers and provide information unique to the candidate.

Personal information such as hobbies and interests should not be included on the resume unless there is significant white space at the end of the resume or it could provide additional support for interest in a future career choice.

Resumes in the past just contained shorthand job descriptions. Recruiters seek more information. They are looking for candidates who *fit* their current open position and their company. Providing accomplishments on the resume ensures your resume will be reviewed.

Accomplishment Description

In today's market, the savvy job seeker will provide information about their accomplishments and skills in a quantitative manner. Placing a few well descriptive accomplishments throughout the resume will showcase or highlight the job seeker's experience.

> Good Example: *Quality Control Manager in charge of seven member technician team*
>
> Best Example: *Quality Control Manager led seven member team to achieve 15% cost savings through reduction of returned materials*

This resume will get noticed. That's the main difference between just listing job duties and providing them along with job accomplishments. Anyone can list job responsibilities but stating accomplishments will set the candidate at a higher level. Recruiters need individuals who have specific credentials and industry knowledge, but with that, look for those who show they can solve problems and get results. Job seekers who list accomplishments demonstrate these skills. Be judicious with accomplishments. A few specific, well-placed accomplishments are better than listing all of them.

These accomplishments should be:

- Concise
- Have meaning and
- Be applicable to the position job description

The more pertinent the content of the resume, the better for the job seeker. This is where someone who has 25 years of experience can create a two-page or even one-page resume designed specifically for a position by focusing their experience and knowledge in the most germane areas.

List major accomplishments in your resume

Resume Styles

There are three traditional styles of resumes: chronological, functional and curriculum vitae.

A. Chronological

These resumes list candidate's experience from the present to the past. Jobs and the accomplishments and responsibilities comprise the majority of these resumes.

B. Functional

These resumes highlight specific skill sets as employment headers, such as Accounting, Web Design, Management, Supply Management, Project Management, etc. Employers are usually listed in short one-liners under an "Employers" heading.

C. Curriculum vitae

These are used by educators and scientists (not discussed in this guide.)

Using word processing software, it is feasible and highly recommended to tailor the resume for each position. This allows the job seeker to highlight skills, credentials or information pertinent for the particular position. Many company website gather facts about the work history as part of the submission process, therefore having a resume which highlights skill sets or accomplishments in a quantifiable manner provides more detailed information.

Most recruiters like to see a resume start with an objective. It should be:

- short
- specific
- succinct

Poor Exp: Work in an environment that allows me to creatively express my true talent

Good Exp: Team member in the audit department

When applying for a specific position, place position title or a close proximity of it in the objective line. If you place a specific company name in job objective such as: Engineering Manager for ABC Enterprises, only use this resume for that company. Company recruiters dismiss candidates when a mismatched resume is attached or given. Many take it as a sign of poor organizational skills or poor attention to detail.

> *I was recruiting pilots for regional jet service at USAirways. We received several hundred resumes for these openings. Most of the individuals had put "Pilot for USAirways" as their objective although there was one who had sent in a resume with the following objective: "Pilot for Delta Airlines." Needless to say, this resume went directly into the "circular file."*

A professional resume should be easy to read.
You only have **one** chance to make a good **first** impression.

Easy to Read

- Lots of white space

- Good size margins of an inch or more

- Headings, large and easy to spot

- Job title/descriptions/accomplishments should flow together

- Name and contact information should be noticeable but not overbearing   (Usually 2 to 4 font sizes above text size)

- No personal information – no pictures – no hobbies

- Appropriate professional candidate email address

Action words
powerfully
convey experience

Action Words

Resume sentences are written in phrases and begin with action words. Keep in mind that your finished resume should only be one or two pages long. Action words powerfully convey skills, experience, and education. Action words can help develop concise, descriptive sentences.

Review the accompanying list of action words on the next page, and incorporate them into your resume using the following guidelines:

- As the resume subject, delete the pronoun "I" and begin sentences with action words.

- Develop an active tone which projects initiative rather than participation. This is achieved by using either the present or past tense for action words. Be cautious of action words ending in "ing," which denote participation.

- Use a higher level of diction, if appropriate. For example, it maybe more effective to say "authored" instead of "wrote."

- Keep phrases in a bulleted section parallel. If you begin phrases with action words, all of the phrases should begin the same way. Do not mix phrases starting with action words and nouns.

- Keep tenses consistent. When writing a chronological resume, duties for a current position should be in the present tense and previous positions in the past tense. For a functional resume, the tense should be consistent throughout the resume.

Action Words

accelerate	control	formulate	originate	retrieve
accomplish	converted	found	outline	review
achieve	coordinate	generate	participate	revise
acquired	correspond	guide	persuade	schedule
adapted	create	handle	plan	select
administered	counsel	identify	prepare	serve
adjust	defined	illustrate	present	set-up
advise	delegate	implement	process	shape
advocate	demonstrate	improve	produce	share
altered	design	improvised	programmed	simplify
analyze	devise	increase	proofread	sold
approve	develop	initiate	propose	solicit
assemble	direct	innovate	protect	solve
assessed	dispense	inspect	provide	staff
authored	distribute	install	publicize	streamline
balance	draft	instituted	publish	strengthen
budgeted	drive	introduce	purchase	structured
built	earn	invent	raise	study
changed	edit	inventoried	recommend	succeed
collaborate	eliminate	investigate	record	summarized
collect	enable	launch	recruit	supervise
communicate	encourage	led	redesign	systematized
compare	entertain	manage	reduce	synthesize
compiled	establish	marketed	refer	theorized
completed	estimate	mediate	regulate	track
composed	evaluate	mentor	reinforce	transform
computed	examine	monitor	reorganize	translate
conceive	exceed	motivate	repair	trim
conduct	execute	navigate	replicate	tutor
configured	expand	negotiate	report	unite
consolidate	fabricate	obtain	represent	update
construct	facilitate	operate	research	utilize
contacted	figured	order	resolve	verify
contribute	forecast	organize	retain	volunteer

Editing Guidelines

- ❧ Use a dictionary to check spelling, hyphenation, correct usage, and capitalization

- ❧ Use only acronyms and abbreviations clearly understood by the general population (When writing acronyms, generally use all uppercase letters and also check for the use of a period to punctuate some abbreviations)

- ❧ Use adjectives with caution since they show a degree of comparison and, if overused, can clutter communication and obscure your message (Example: *highly* technical. The word highly clutters communication and is hard to define.)

- ❧ Colons used in headings are usually redundant and should be avoided

Additional Resume Guidelines

Have an objective – short, less than seven words

One page is best

Sentences brief and concise

Easy to read – easy on eyes

Over age 50 – limit job history to the last 10 to 15 years

Have more than one resume – craft resume for each job

Have electronic resumes: scannable / email / text

*Create an electronic resume
that can be easily
customized for each position*

Electronic Resumes

Most job seekers today create their professional resume using a software program which presents a professional presence. Having a resume in this format is wonderful since it can be saved and then edited for specific applications.

One application is the creation of a truly "electronic" version. Some companies only accept on-line applications and resumes. They no longer retain paper copies. Having a clean, easy-to-read electronic resume is a must for today's job seeker.

Another plus for an electronic resume is the amount of additional information that can be given to an employer. Since many of the company specific job sites gather information about employment history, this allows the job seeker to highlight skills and accomplishments on the resume rather than just list job responsibilities.

The electronic version has three forms: scannable, email or plain text versions.

A. Scannable

Scannable resumes are used by most companies today to keep a record of a candidate's resume. Scannable resumes should be easy to read with no special fonts or formatting. They are not "pretty" but very functional. Some companies do not even accept paper resumes while others may take the paper resume, scan it into their system for electronic storage/recovery and then recycle the paper copy.

These resumes may also be read by software looking for industry or job-related keywords. Keywords may include software programs, such MS for MicroSoft, SAS, AutoCAD or terms used by specific departments such as CQI, Six Sigma, and LEAN for quality control. Please include these words on your resume sparingly. Other terms such as CD may have several meanings, such as Compact Disk or Certificate of Deposit. With too many keywords, the resume will not make sense and the recruiter will be suspicious.

B. Email

An email resume is used in the body of an email. Please make sure the resume "fits" the line restriction formatting for this type of correspondence. This usually means shorter text lines, spacing between sections, text-based highlighting and no paragraphs. Adding the resume as an attachment only gives the recruiter/hiring manager a reason for not reading it since it requires additional time and effort to open up an attachment. Having it in the body of the email gives the reader instant access to your information and credentials. Please note: An email message can be deleted in the blink of an eye. Give them a professional reason to look – not push delete.

C. Plain Text

Plain text resumes can also be used by scanning machines but are mainly used to copy and paste into on-line job applications or on-line job databases.

Internet Resume Guidelines

In the 21st century, it is important for every job seeker to utilize the tools and services available on the internet. Many companies only accept resumes and applications thru their on-line portal. Using the following tips and techniques will set you above you competition.

A. Candidates should have a professional email address. Initials and last name or last name with numbers is most appropriate. Recruiters will instantly dismiss candidates whose email address is something like: sexylover@hotmail.com or thebest@yahoo.com.

Have a professional email address

B. Apply to specific company job websites – limit submissions to 3 or less per website. Recruiters can determine how many times an individual has applied for different positions. Corporate recruiters usually stay away from someone who has applied for over 5 positions on their company website.

C. "Blasting" is putting your resume anywhere and everywhere on the web. "Blasting" your resume is not appreciated by most recruiters and they usually stay away from those individuals who do "blast."

D. Use professional websites, such as those for accounting, engineering, etc., to review their listing of current opportunities (American Society of Mechanical Engineers, Society of Human Resource Professionals, American Institute of Certified Public Accountants, American Association of University Women, etc.) These sites usually have fewer visitors so by responding to their listings, the number of applicants is smaller and your resume may stand out more.

E. Using only large job boards (Monster, CareerBuilder, etc) severely limits job search and may offer too much exposure. There have also been security breaches involving member personal information such as passwords and other data in the past.

F. Carefully consider how much information to share with the world and which sites to use. Some sites keep all information private while others may sell their "lists" to third parties. If there is not a "confidential" statement, then consider all information posted to that website as available to the world.

G. Always double check information before you "click." Confirm appropriate resume is attached before hitting the "send" button.

H. Jobs in the federal government sector are listed at www.usa-jobs.opm.gov website. It is the resource for federal jobs.

I. Keep a log of all the positions, companies and websites along with application date. Please remember to delete all information once a job has been obtained. Information in cyberspace has a way of taking on a life of its' own. If the corporate recruiter found you once in cyberspace, they can find you again. *Do you want to tell your new boss you forgot to delete your file?*

J. Clean up any personal information on MySpace.com, Face-Book.com, Twitter.com or any site where personal information is accessible. During the job search, projecting a professional image is a must. Some recruiters I know scan these sites for candidate information as well. (Note: There have been several recent articles concerning information posted on websites. Some items never go away even after they have been deleted.)

K. Please note - Jobs posted on a website may be out of date (if job has been posted for 3 months or more – it could be filled or they could be having a very hard time filling this position.)

L. Conduct a "Google" search of your name. See what information is out there.

There are just a few of the items to consider when using this electronic medium. For those job seekers who are using this medium for the first time, do not get discouraged when there is no response to your submittal or application. This is standard operating procedure in the job market today. Most companies will let you know at the end of the submittal if you were successful in the transmission of your data but that is usually the extent of the feedback. Electronic resumes are normally kept on-file between six to twelve months in their company database.

There is a lot more to it than just "posting" your resume. The savvy job seeker will look to capitalize their experience and expertise in this electronic media while maintaining privacy and exclusivity.

The World Wide Web is a tool.
- Use it wisely -

Cover Letters

Since many companies today only have electronic submission of resumes through their website portal, cover letters have diminished in use. However, cover letters are still appropriate and, when used correctly, can enhance a job seeker's opportunities. Many small businesses (where most of America is employed) accept and even, expect a cover letter with a resume. It is an important marketing tool and can help get your resume reviewed. (*See example in Appendix N*)

The cover letter should have at least three paragraphs:

First paragraph:

The beginning sentence explains why you are writing the letter and expresses your interest in the position. Where you saw the ad or opportunity listed, how you learned of the position or who suggested they might have an opening. It is short and brief. It should be two to three sentences at most.

Second paragraph:

This is the core of the letter. "*What's in it for them?*" Why should they look at your resume? Describe how your skills and knowledge can benefit the company. Select only two to three attributes or qualifications. Give them something **extra** not listed on the resume. Equate a past accomplishment to their work environment. This is an opportunity for you to give them a reason to contact you about the position.

Third paragraph:

The end of the letter should be optimistic. Thank them for reviewing your information and suggest a follow-up, such as: "*I will be contacting you next week to discuss . . .*" This paragraph should be brief and concise as well.

With many companies utilizing email for both internal and external correspondence, an excellent cover letter could showcase your excellent written communication skills. Don't miss an opportunity to display your skills.

BEST FOOT FORWARD

Cover Letter Guidelines

- Address letter to a specific person

- Review for grammatical errors; use a dictionary to check spelling, punctuation, etc.

- Use "I" and "me" sparingly (Avoid starting each sentence with a personal pronoun)

- Use action verbs so tone is more persuasive

- One page

- Provide contact information in an easy-to-read format

Phone Interview

During the time you are looking for a job –

Always answer the phone with a smile on your face.

If it is not a good time to answer the phone – don't!

Having a smile will present a pleasant voice and a good **first** impression over the phone.

Phone interviews are usually the first interface with a prospective company. Most companies conduct a phone screen to determine if more time and effort should be invested in the candidate. A phone screen is one method recruiters use to determine which candidates to invite to the next round or take off their list. It is a screening. Think of the recruiter as a gatekeeper. After the phone interview, you may be asked in or you may be shut out. At this point, the good news is – you have a phone interview.

When you are asked to participate in a phone interview, allow time for the interview and conduct it in a quiet place.

- Be sure to have your resume, cover letter, employment history, and any other documentation you may need within easy reach.

- Have pen and paper handy so you can record the name of the interviewer, the time and the company.

- Take notes during the interview.

- Hold the phone to hear and be heard.

- If you have a bad connection and are experiencing difficulty in hearing, inform the recruiter and ask them to call you back.

While you may be sitting in your pajamas, project a professional image over the phone by maintaining your posture, keeping your shoulders and back straight. I know of job seekers who "dressed" for a phone interview because it kept them in the proper frame of mind. They did not want to get too comfortable during the interview and say something improper.

This is one place where effective listening skills are very important. Remaining calm and focusing on the recruiter's questions will help guide your thoughts and answers to the task at hand.

Always answer the phone
with a smile on your face!

Interviewing

An interview is the corporate standard for evaluating potential employees. The purpose of the interview is to exchange information between the recruiter and the candidate. It is the recruiter's responsibility to ask the questions. The interview is meant to be a conversation with a purpose.

Recruiter's Purpose: Determine if job seeker has the knowledge, qualifications, skills and interest for the position.

Match with company culture.

Job Seekers' Purpose: Provide information on knowledge, qualifications, skills and interest in the position.

Obtain additional job information and observe employees

Receive job offer

During an interview, the goal is to *fit in* not make a personal statement. The overall purpose of the interview is to get a job offer. Once an offer has been extended, a decision can be made whether or not it is the one for you.

Be prepared for a variety of interviewing questions. Do not wing it! Recruiters equate how well someone conducts themselves in an interview to how well a candidate will function in the work place. If a candidate is prepared and well spoken, then recruiters believe these characteristics will be transferred to the workplace as well.

Recruiters have a problem, a job opening, and they are looking for a solution, a specific solution, the best individual for the job. The candidate must present themselves as the best solution.

There is a variety of interviewing techniques companies employ for this phase of the job search process. Some of these techniques include using:

- Standard interview questions

- Behavioral based interviewing

- Competency-based interviewing

- Combination of above techniques

- No specific process – wing it

The job seeker must be prepared for any and all of the above interviewing techniques. Let's start with the most basic of those questions. These questions, while general in nature, help fill in the gaps or provide general information about the job seeker. The following questions are usually asked sometimes during the interview process.

Standard Interview Questions

Standard or typical questions for any position include: (*Questions and Answers are in Appendix L*)

a. Tell me about yourself.

b. What are your strengths?

c. What are your weaknesses?

d. What do you like most about your current / former position?

e. What do you like least about your current / former position?

f. Why are you leaving your present job?

g. Why should we hire you?

h. What would your former boss(es) say about your performance?

i. What is your ideal job or career?

j. How has your education prepared you for this position or your career?

k. What do you know about our company?

l. What salary amount are you looking for?

How to Answer

The candidate should answer questions succinctly. Your answers should be:

- ❧ Short
- ❧ Concise and
- ❧ Informative.

Most interview questions can be answered in sixty seconds or less. If the interviewer would like more information, they will ask.

Provide specific examples of your actions or thoughts, give numbers or quantify the problem, actions and solution. Utilize the behavioral-based interviewing model. (More information in following section)

Don't be emotional. This is especially true for job seekers who are going through a career transition. Most companies have experienced some measure of layoffs, job elimination or other employment controls in the past few years. Be prepared to give positive examples of what you have learned or accomplished through this experience. This will go a long way in showing how you have handled adversity. Some interviewers will intentionally or unintentionally create an emotional situation. Do not go there. **When emotions enter an interview, success leaves.**

Listen to the question and think before you answer. It is good to anticipate the questions but sometimes, we can misinterpret what someone is asking or we may be stumped by a question. Learn to give yourself time to answer a question. If you need a little more time to think about your answer, let the interviewer know, "*That's an interesting question, let me think which example would best answer that question.*" or if you did not hear the question completely, have a follow-up question to ask, such as: "*Can you clarify what you are asking?*"

Most people only think about the talking part when interviewing is discussed but a major part of the interview is listening. Listening, *truly listening*, is really hard work. Trying to maintain your focus and energy requires concentration and determination. Effective listening requires focusing not only on the dialog but the content of the dialog as well.

An interview is more than just a conversation. The job seeker is:

a. **a detective**: seeking clues about the position and the organization.

b. **a marketer**: selling your skills and expertise to obtain a position.

The **effective** job seeker will stay focused on the discussion and the questions while an **ineffective** job seeker will zone out or miss part of the interview.

Any professional recruiter can spot a candidate whose mind has *left the building*. For most recruiters, this becomes the time for the candidate to physically leave the building.

Always prepare for any interview

Behavioral-based Interviewing

Many companies use behavioral-based interviewing techniques. It is one tool used to help ensure consistent, reliable hiring decisions are made. It is built upon the premise that past performance and behavior helps predict future performance and behavior.

Behavioral interviewing employs the use of behavioral questions. Behavioral questions request the candidate to talk about their behavior or actions in the past. During an interview, candidates are asked questions about their past experiences, both positive and negative, to determine if their behavior, knowledge, skills and accomplishments match with the job description, competencies and company's current culture.

Recruiters will gather specific examples of a candidate's past actions rather than identify general traits or other subjective criteria. I call this information, a behavioral instance. This is solicited from the candidate's past experiences and accomplishments in conjunction with the circumstances surrounding those experiences. The interviewer is looking for three specific components which make up the behavioral instance:

- **Assignment**
- **Behavior**
- **Consequences**

Behavioral questions are explained in greater detail in the next section.

This information is recorded on a consistent, specifically designed questionnaire.

The final step in this process is the evaluation of the candidate's answer. This is the most critical step since all hiring decisions will be made based upon this step. Decision points are clearly defined and, in most cases, there is a group consensus for the hiring decision. This helps ensure all candidates are treated fairly and equally.

One of the best interview sessions I conducted was with Suzanne. She was interviewing for a marketing specialist in our Sales & Marketing group. Suzanne was currently working as a marketing professional for a major corporation in our area.

She walked into the interview with a smile on her face and confidence in her step. From her current position, she knew the major competencies of the position. She had come prepared. She had brought samples of her work: a workbook and slide presentation for a marketing campaign she had developed and successful implemented.

No doubt about it, Suzanne knew about behavioral-based interviewing and she was ready for our questions. Her interview went extremely well. She was invited back for our final round of interviews and she was offered the position.

BEST FOOT FORWARD

Behavioral-based Components

The company develops the interviewing questions and the questionnaire. It is up to the candidate to answer the questions. In behavioral-based interviewing, a candidate is considered to have successfully answered the question when they provide a "complete" behavioral instance. A complete behavioral instance is formed by these three components:

1. **Assignment,** *Project or Problem the candidate was involved in*

2. **Behavior of the candidate**

3. **Consequences,** *Outcomes or Results of those actions*

   *(Remember your **A**, **B**, **C**'s)*

The candidate needs to be ready to answer questions in this format and in this order. This is not as easy as it seems. Most of us begin at the end. For example, a recruiter may say, "*Tell me about a time you were involved in a team project.*"

> Job seeker's normal answer: "*Oh, most of my projects are team projects.*"
>
> Savvy job seeker's answer: "*I've been involved in a variety of team projects. One of my most memorable was working on new software interface project. There were four of us on the team. We had to create, test and implement this interface in six months.*
>
> *I took the lead as communications liaison which involved working with our in-house IT staff, our executive team and the software vendor to help insure we were in compliance and on-target with the interface's objectives. I was responsible for coordinating our weekly meetings, confirming attendance and editing the project report.*
>
> *Based upon my reporting details, the vendor authorized more people to the project. This helped us not only get the project done earlier than expected but we came in under budget as well.*"

89

A knowledgeable job seeker will be able to create a variety of behavioral-based scenarios based upon their work experience. To help you create these scenarios, let's take a more in-depth view of the three components for behavioral-based answers. (Use Appendix B to record your scenarios.)

Assignment, *Project or Problem*

The assignment, project or problem provides the backdrop from which to solicit information on the behavior of the candidate. In behavioral-based questions, this needs to be illustrated. By illustrating the assignment, the candidate helps the recruiter to understand and appreciate the accomplishments achieved. Usual assignments, projects or problems arise from the following situations:

    a. Candidate's past job objectives or responsibilities

    b. Changes in the candidate's job responsibilities or work processes

    c. Team projects

    d. Special requests from a manager or customer

    e. Challenges in meeting a deadline

    f. Difficulty in working with a co-worker

    g. Significant problem encountered

Behavior

Behaviors provide information on what the candidate has done or said. Behaviors are usually implied but in behavioral-based interviewing, recruiters will ask candidates to describe, detail or define their actions. This helps the recruiter determine "what" the candidate does or "how" they react in situations. Most candidates have trouble defining their specific behavior or actions especially when working in a team environment but it is crucial for the candidate to help the recruiter understand what actions they specifically took. Recruiters are looking for candidates who take action and work to get tasks done. They are not looking for someone who has all the answers rather someone who has demonstrated the ability to get the answers. Some examples of behavior or action are:

    a. How a work plan was developed and followed

    b. How a work assignment was completed

    c. How a particular tight deadline was met (or not)

    d. What an individual said or did that caused a co-worker to become angry

    e. What an individual did when a major problem was encountered

Consequences, *Outcomes or Results*

Consequences are the accomplishments, outcomes or results of behaviors. They tell the recruiter what changes or difference the candidate's behavior made and whether the actions were effective, appropriate or unsuccessful. Some examples of consequences are:

    a. Budget was met

    b. Project was completed on time

    c. Project was not completed on time and steps taken to improve outcome

    d. Major goal was accomplished

    e. Major goal not accomplished and steps taken to improve outcome

    f. Certification

    g. Promotion

In and of themselves, accomplishments can be very impressive. However, to fully understand their significance, the recruiter will request the assignment (circumstances) and the behavior (actions) leading to those results.

In behavioral-based questions, recruiters need information about a candidate's behavior in a specific situation. If the words, "*I usually . . .*" start your answer, then try again and this time state a specific situation, what actions you took and what were the consequences. It is crucial in the behavioral-based method of interviewing to give your answers always in the proper order. Without the three components in order, the interviewer may not be able to effectively evaluate your experience.

Just remember your A, B, C's!

Sample Behavioral-based Interviewing Questions

- Tell me about a situation where you had to assume the leadership role

- Tell me about a time you employed your creativity

- Describe a situation where you had to adjust quickly to a change due to time, budget or organizational priorities.

- Describe the most difficult person you had to work with and detail your actions.

- What do you consider the most important contribution your previous department made to your organization, and what was your role in that contribution?

Evaluation (Compiled after the interview)

The evaluation of the candidate is done after the job seeker has left the building. In behavioral-based interviewing, the evaluation is conducted by looking at each interview question and determining how well the candidate answered it using a complete behavioral-based answer.

> *One of my most memorable and worst interviews was with Sam. I truly believe he thought he was the answer to any corporation's need. He entered the room as if he was the captain in command of a ship. There was no doubt in my mind, and certainly in Sam's, he acted as if he had the job already.*
>
> *From his resume, I believed Sam was an intelligent and competent man. After our initial greeting and general set-up, I began the interview using our behavioral-based interview questionnaire for our sales manager position. (I had also reviewed his resume. He had listed three jobs with three different employers in the past five years.) I began the interview, "Congratulations on the DeGuire award. Tell me a little bit about it and why it was given to you." He looked at me with a supercilious smile and a twinkle in his eye and said, "They always give it to the new Sales Manager at the end of their first year. I just completed my first year."*
>
> *I continued to ask Sam to expand on his work experience and received little information about his specific actions. During our evaluation process, it became apparent Sam had provided very few details on his accomplishments or specific skills to anyone. He talked more about what he wanted to accomplish than what he had done.*
>
> **Result:** He was not asked for a second interview.

Competency-Based Interviewing

The focus of competency-based interviewing is the job and the requirements, or competencies, for the job. Competency-based interview questions are generated from the skill set or competencies required for the position. This technique utilizes the competencies of the position to help determine if there is a *fit* between the candidate and the position. Incorporating behavior-based questions based upon the position competencies provides the recruiter with concrete information to make an informed decision versus going with a "gut feel." Competencies for any job may be divided into three types of skill sets. The three skill sets are defined as:

a. **Specific abilities or content skills**, such as software knowledge, degree appropriate knowledge, etc

b. **Functional or transferable skills**, such as organizational skills, time management skills, communication skills, planning, etc

c. **Self-management, adaptive skills or personal characteristic skills**, such as team player, integrity, reliable, work standards, etc.

(Appendix H provides an opportunity to list your unique skill sets.)

Common competencies for many professional jobs are:

- Teamwork
- Communication skills
- Flexibility, etc.

Other competencies will be more job-specific such as:

- Software skills for a graphic artist
- Management skills for supervisor,
- Language skills for customer service, sales, public relations, etc.

Common competencies for management positions are:

- Managing people and teams
- Managing conflict or conflict resolution
- Leadership skills

However, if you do not know the specific competencies for a particular position, research has shown the top five skills in corporate America are:

- Oral communication
- Creativity
- Ability to work in a team
- Written communication
- Technical ability

Technical ability pertains to the specific college degree, certification, technical knowledge or know-how needed for the position such as:

- Engineering, Accounting and IT degrees
- Software certifications
- Welding certifications

Asking for a job description before the interview would be very helpful. In most cases, the major competencies or skills are listed in the position advertisement. Knowing the skills or competencies required for a position is very helpful when preparing for an interview. If you are applying for a similar position to your last one, you should have a very good idea of these competencies.

Sample Competency-based Interviewing Questions

- ❧ Describe an assignment that stretched your technical expertise

- ❧ How do you determine whether you have met your customer's expectations?

- ❧ Describe some decisions you made without all of the pertinent information.

- ❧ Describe a situation where you recommended an approach which was very different from how your company has operated in the past.

Just as the hiring decision will be made on how well the candidate conducts themselves in the interview and if the candidate is the best fit for the position, the candidate must make the ultimate career decision – "Do I want to work here or not?" Give yourself the best possible opportunity to answer that question. Let's look at questions you should ask to make a better informed job decision.

Research show 85% of job success is successfully applying people skills.

Questions Candidates Can Ask

As stated earlier, it is the interviewer's responsibility to ask the questions. Ninety-five percent of the interview is controlled by the interviewer. The other five percent, a candidate must use to their advantage. It is an opportunity for the candidate to ask questions, understand the culture, job requirement, etc. This information will be used by the candidate to evaluate their fit within a particular company or organization.

Recruiters want candidates who ask pertinent questions. The candidate must be prepared for both human resource recruiters as well as interviews with the manager or peers of the position. It's crucial that you have several questions prepared to ask during the interview. Generally, the number of questions asked about the position and the company during the interview is used to measure your level of interest in the position. If you don't ask any questions, you'll give the interviewer the impression that you're either not very interested or not well prepared for the interview.

Most interviewers will tell you when you will have an opportunity to ask questions. Usually it's at the end of the interview. However, sometimes you may be asked if you have any questions at the beginning of the interview. I would strongly suggest keeping your questions to the end of the interview: just tell the interviewer, *"I would rather save my questions to the end since the interview may answer some on my questions."*

Once the interviewer has given you specific information about the position, emphasize your key qualifications for the job and bring up qualities that haven't been mentioned yet. Notice a number of these questions, listed on the next page, gives you another opportunity to sell yourself. Tie your qualifications into what the interviewer has just told you about the position, department, or organization.

Questions the job seeker might ask are:

- What is the most important skill required in this position?

- Why is this position open? / Why has this position become vacant?

- What are some of the other responsibilities of this job?

- With whom will I be working most often?

- What do you think are the specific challenges of this position?

- What are the projected strategic goals for the organization? For the department?

- What type of performance evaluation is used by your organization?

- What qualities do you look for in a potential employee?

- What resources would I have responsibility for in this position?

- How do you measure success?

- How quickly would you need the successful candidate on board after you make your hiring decision?

Questions the job seeker should never ask *in an interview* are:

- What does your company do?

- What does your medical insurance cover?

- How soon can I expect a raise?

- How many smoking breaks can employee take a day?

- What other jobs do you have available?

One of my pet peeves, and all recruiters have them, is changing clothes at the interview site. I understand there are valid reasons for candidates to change their attire. They may have a work uniform and be short on time, have to drive a long distance home, or don't want to wear the suit on the plane, etc.

Find another place to change clothes. From my perspective as a recruiter, I wonder what else may also change. This is one of my quirks. I know, it is a quirk, but . . .

Ask pertinent job-related questions

Interview Pointers

- **Tell the truth** – never provide false information.

- Turn off your cell phone.

- Be sure you understand a question before you answer. If a question catches you by surprise, take a moment to think about it.

- Provide examples to illustrate a point. "*I haven't missed a day of work in four years.*" is stronger than "*I'm depend-able.*"

- Volunteer information only if it's **positive and relevant**.

- **Never complain** about a previous job, boss or com-pany – stay positive!

- Observe the interviewer to determine their level of in-terest in the subject being discussed.

- Look for clues that may reflect the interviewer's inter-ests, personality, values, etc.

- Be alert for opportunities to sell your skills.

Practice Interviewing Skills

Role play the interview with someone who will hold you account-able for your answers - someone who will listen to make sure each answer relates to the specific interview question. This individual may also be able to point out annoying speech patterns (such as saying "*Uh*" when filling in gaps), nervous habits (bouncing knees, twirling pen, etc), disconcerting twitches (eye blinking, teeth clacking, etc) and other personal non-verbal habits. This is a very important element in the interview process and is missed by most candidates. Some candidate may video-tape themselves to review their interactions.

Have an employment counselor -
Someone to act as a "reality" check

When looking for a new position, many job seekers believe in go-ing it alone. Granted most of the work is done by the job seeker, searching for opportunities, researching companies, writing cover letters and resumes, interviewing, etc. However, the savvy job seeker will have a friend who will act as an employment counselor. This counselor is someone whose opinion they value and trust. Some-one who can give positive encouragement but also help the job seeker view situations in a realistic light not as they would like to see them or as they think they are. It is okay to have more than one employment counselor.

> **Example 1:** *Job seeker has gone on three interviews but has not received any offers. He asks his employment counselor to conduct a mock interview and pro-vide feedback about his interviewing skills. Af-ter the mock interview, the employment coun-selor recommends the job seeker take the change*

out of his pant pocket since he juggled the loose coins all during the interview.

(The job seeker has no knowledge of this nervous habit.)

Example 2: *Job seeker wants to apply for position in Oklahoma after living in Pennsylvania for over 50 years. Employment counselor advises against this since job seeker's whole family, including grandchildren, are within a hundred mile radius of his current home and they are a very close knit family.*

First Impressions

How a candidate looks is extremely important since first impressions are typically made within the first ten to twenty seconds. Your name is the most important asset when introducing yourself – say it distinctly. The second most important name is the interviewer's – repeat it during the introduction (*"Pleasure meeting you Mr. Brown."*) and use it during the interview (*"Ms. Jones, I'm glad you asked that question."*) Other tips include:

- Shake hands firmly – interlock hands via the thumbs

- Make friendly eye contact – smile

- Stand tall and proud during the introductions

- Remember the interviewer's name – jot it down

Dress Professionally

Most candidates do not get passed the first interview because they do not dress appropriately. Interviewing for a professional position with Fortune 500 corporations or industries which interface with the public, such as retail or other consumer goods and services, is standard business operations which demand professional attire. The interview apparel should be business appropriate. Business dress, suit and tie for men, suit and blouse for women, is the most common. Be conservative and sincere – wear dark blue. Individuals who wear blue are seen as sincere, reliable and more intelligent. This may be due to many professional service organizations using dark blue or navy uniforms such as Emergency Medical Technicians (EMT's) and police departments. If blue is not your color, then medium to dark grey. Black is too harsh and brown is too earthly (just for interviewing purposes.)

Suits should be comfortable with room to move. Most men and women look more professional and at ease when their clothes are "loose" and flatter the body shape instead of clothes which "mold" or "act as a griddle" to keep the shape in. Women should also be aware of the length of their suits or dresses. Tugging at the hemline to make them longer during the interview will be noted, usually in the negative. Interviewers should be focused on the candidate's skills and knowledge for the position rather than wondering if the buttons on the candidate's shirt are going to pop off or if the hemline is suddenly going to grow by three inches. This is a job interview, not a dating service.

Cologne or perfume is discouraged due to allergies or unknown reactions from others. (Your perfume could be their ex's favorite.)

Body art and jewelry is an individuals' form of expression and its' use and taste is subject to individual preferences. If possible, cover up any body art, wear long sleeves or pants. Body piecing should be kept to a minimum – one set of earrings in the ears for women, none for men. *(Please keep in mind: the objective during a job interview is to blend in – not make a fashion or lifestyle statement.)*

Poise and Confidence

Attitude is everything. Having a positive, confident and winning attitude is essential in the job search process. Looking for a job is a job and it may take time. There will be rejections so a thick skin is needed.

Be calmly assertive, there is a fine line between a healthy positive attitude and a monster ego. An individual with a positive attitude comes across as someone who can accomplish goals while working well with others. They are sincerely confident of their skills and abilities. They have a keen sense of their value to their future company. In fact, having a positive attitude opens up the creative and constructive thinking capability with the expectation of success. There is a subliminal sense of optimism that is contagious.

Emotions must also be kept under control. Recruiters have a finely tuned antenna. Emotional states are very easy for recruiters to gauge. Becoming overly emotional during the interview is not a good thing. Please see the section - *Desperation Is Not An Option.* It is good to be passionate about your work but during the interview staying calm and professional is the best way to impress a recruiter.

Positive affirmations or statements can be helpful in creating a positive, confident and assured presence. Using positive affirmations create new mental patterns which in turn affects our physical and emotional being. Successful affirmations employ two focusing techniques, intention and expectation. Intention refers to a result, purpose or end. It is what we "*want to be.*" Expectation deals with believing we have received our intention. The key to using positive affirmations is to do so *with* action –the key word being *action.* Action is planned personal behavior. It is this action which will bring the affirmation to fruition. From my personal experience, if no action is taken on the affirmation, you are wasting your time and breath.

Brain researchers have found the brain does not differentiate between "imaging" something to actually "doing" something *if you imagine it clearly, strongly and consistently.* This is backed up by sports researchers who have found that over 80% of athletes use some form of mental imagery to enhance performance, such as basketball players imaging shooting successful free throws. Australian psychologist Allen Richardson conducted an experiment investigating the power of the mind utilizing basketball players. He divided the players into three groups:

- Group 1 – practiced shooting baskets for 20 minutes a day,

- Group 2 – did not practice at all and

- Group 3 – mentally rehearsed shooting baskets for 20 minutes a day.

At the end of the study, he found Group 1 had the most improvement. Group 2 had no improvement. Surprisingly, Group 3 had improved almost as well as Group 1 *without ever touching* a basketball.

The mind is a powerful tool. Affirmations can ignite this power; then, actions feed the power. Just as a fire needs fuel to burn, affirmations radiate when actions are implemented.

So if your affirmation is, "I am poised and confident," you will see yourself as poised and confident. Actions to help reinforce this affirmation would be: lifting your head high and keeping your shoulders square and relaxed while walking confidently. Your body language projects a positive image reinforcing your affirmation.

These affirmations will help during the tough times, when you have to make the phone call to a prospective employer or when you receive negative news. Staying positive and focused is hard work.

Nervous Habits

Talking with your hands, playing with your hair, adjusting your neck tie signals someone who is nervous or has a lack of confidence. Be aware of your nervous tendencies and rein them in during the interview.

Keep your hands relaxed. Hold the left wrist with the right hand or keep one hand on the table if available. Don't cross your arms. Take notes, if appropriate, but make sure to refer to them during the interview. Crossing your legs may be appropriate but make sure your posture is not compromised nor your modesty. Do not bounce the knees up and down. On the other side, do not become *so* relaxed that you ease your sitting position or lace your hands behind your head (this is usually done by men versus women). Chewing gum or smoking should never be done while on the company's premises.

Your every move is being watched and recorded either on paper or mentally.

Ask your employment counselor to conduct an informal or mock interview to determine what nervous habits you may have. *(As an outplacement consultant, I've had many job seekers reveal these habits during a mock interview.)*

Once you know what these nervous habits are, you can take steps to correct or eliminate them.

Cell Phone Etiquette

Never have your cell phone on during the interview process. This starts when you enter the building and ends when you leave the building. If you are meeting at a restaurant, turn the cell off once you have met the interviewer. Even during a phone interview at home, turn off the cell phone if you are using a land line for the interview. A cell phone that is ringing or vibrating can be distracting.

All your attention should be on the interviewer and the task at hand!

*Turn off cell phone
when interviewing*

Please check out www.nothired.com for more information on *what not to do* during an interview or through the job search process. At this website, recruiters provide stories of their personal experience in working with candidates. (*Just a word to the wise.*)

Desperation is Not an Option

Professional recruiters sense the energy a candidate projects. They can sense individuals who are desperate. Desperate job seekers convey they want a job, *any* job and *can do any* job.

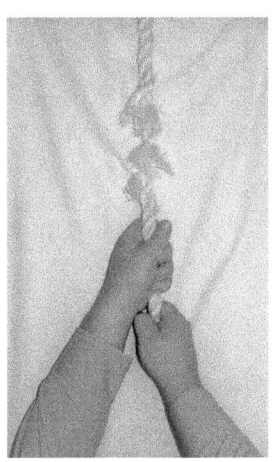

Companies do not want and will not hire someone who is desperate. Desperate individuals come across as being emotionally unstable and unprofessional. Recruiters will run, not walk, away from "desperate" candidates.

Take any *needy or whining* inflection out of your voice, face and body. This is an instant interview killer for the recruiter.

> *One of my shortest interviews was with Steven. I asked him, "Why should the company hire you for this position?" His answer was, "He needed the job to support his family."*
>
> *Unfortunately, Steve chose an inappropriate answer to my question. He did not get the job. He should have focused on his abilities and skills to perform the functions of the job, his past performance, his accomplishments and how they relate to this present position.*

Recruiters and managers are looking for an individual with a specific skill set not someone who is a "jack of all trades and master of none." Candidates who believe they can do any job are fooling only themselves.

You know you are desperate:

When you start responding to *any* employment ad.

When you interview for a job, *any job*.

When you start to hyperventilate at the thought of never finding a job.

When you want to kick the paperboy because there are not any new employment ads in the paper.

When you want to throw your laptop out the window.

When you look at a career change just because there seems to be more opportunities elsewhere.

When *(you fill in the blank)*

BEST FOOT FORWARD

Not Your New Best Friend

It is the recruiter's responsibility to put the job seeker at ease. This helps facilitate the interview process. Unfortunately, it may not bode well for the job seeker. Becoming too familiar with the recruiter or interviewer may allow the job seeker to say or do something that could jeopardize the possibility of a job offer.

One question recruiters *innocently* ask is "*Did you have any trouble getting here?*" Never answer in the negative. Don't talk about the amount of traffic, how much time it took, difficulty in finding, poor directions, lousy website, etc. This is not the time to *share confidential or negative* observations.

Remain positive and polished – this is a professional business meeting.

Guidelines When Working with a Recruiter

- Treat them with professional courtesy

- Provide them with accurate information

- State strengths confidently

- It is a professional relationship NOT your new best friend

- Share "concerns" sparingly or as appropriate and necessary

Note: Refrain from alcohol during any job search activity. This includes informational meetings, lunch or dinner interviews, and casual meetings with a head hunter or personal recruiter. The time to drink is at a celebration dinner with your friends and family *after* you have accepted the job offer.

BEST FOOT FORWARD

Salary

It is important to talk about salary at the *appropriate* time in the job interview process.

Before the interview:

- Know how much you need to maintain an acceptable standard of living

- Conduct research on salaries for your field, based on various organizations and experience, use websites such as salary.com, expertsalary.com and naceweb.org (entry-level, new college graduates)

- Project a salary range

During the interview:

- Never be the first one to mention a salary figure, and salary should not be mentioned until the end of the interview process

- Try to determine whether a salary offer is fixed or contains room for negotiation

The only time to negotiate a salary is before the offer is accepted.

113

The job seeker is cautioned not to talk about a specific salary until the **following** conditions have been fulfilled:

- ❧ Know exactly what the job entails
- ❧ Found out how well you match the job requirements
- ❧ Knowledge of salary range
- ❧ In the final interview stage
- ❧ Decided you really would like to work there
- ❧ The company has said they want you

Prior to meeting all of the above conditions, it is too early; after you have accepted an offer: it is too late.

After the Interview

Thank-You Letter

Always write a thank-you letter to the interviewer(s) no later than 5 days after the interview. It won't take long. It's a positive step towards impressing the interviewer(s) that is often overlooked.

The thank-you letter can also provide additional selling points of your potential. If there was anything about the interview that left a weak or inaccurate impression, you can try to resolve it in the letter. You might mention a key fact that was left out or expand on your qualifications.

The thank you letter contains a maximum of four short paragraphs that achieve these goals:

- Express appreciation for being considered and why you have a strong interest in the job and organization.

- Review your strong points as they relate to the job and repeat what you will do to help the company solve their problems or meet their needs.

- Present any information that might have been overlooked during the interview. Offer to provide additional information if needed.

- Restate the next steps from your notes; that is, who will do what and when or state, *"Looking forward to working with you."*

If you are no longer interested in a position after the interview, you should still send a thank you letter expressing your appreciation for the opportunity to be considered for the job. It will maintain your positive and professional image.

Critique the Process   *(What went well – What to do better next time)*

To help prepare for the next interview, think back and evaluate the interview experience. Conduct this evaluation as soon as possible after the interview to record things correctly.

Ask yourself:

- Was I on time?

- Did I relate to the interviewer?

- Evaluate the overall interview experience.

- What information did I not convey about myself?

- Did I get answers to all my questions about the job?

- What questions are still unanswered? Be sure to ask them if you're called back for another interview.

- How well did I present the value of my experience?

- How well did I answer questions?

- How well did I communicate verbally?

- What was the best part of my presentation?

- What was the worst?

- Did I come across as confident, shy, aggressive, quiet, nervous, unsure, or eager?

- How could I have improved the interview?

- Did I ask when I'd be hearing from them?

- What will I do to follow up now?

- What is my current status with the company?

- What would be a reason for the company **not** to make an offer?

- Is there anything I can do about it at this point?

- What did I experience that will help me in the next interview?

- How can I do a better job on my next interview?

Learning from the past
will prepare
you for the future.

Fit from the Candidate's Perspective

Fit is also something the candidate should consider as they interact with the company representatives. The purpose of the interview for the job seeker is two-fold:

- ❧ Get a job offer by answering questions, asking for the job and demonstrating how well you ***fit*** the position and the organization

- ❧ Opportunity for you to determine your ***fit*** for the organization

During the interview, the candidate should listen with two perspectives in mind:

1. Demonstrate their skills and abilities to perform the functions of the position and

2. Take notes of job functions for review after the interview.

One of the questions always in the back of the job seeker's mind should be: *"Is this job really the one for me?"* Use the interview time to obtain answers to your questions as well. However, only ask job-related questions, questions concerning the objectives, goals and daily routine of the position. (*Please see section on* **Candidate Questions**) Don't ask questions concerning benefits, such as: time off, vacation schedule, etc. (That time will come - once an offer has been made.)

Questions the candidate should ask themselves about their ***fit*** for the position are:

1. Have I been treated with respect during the hiring process?

2. What is the culture, values and beliefs of the organization? Are they compatible to mine?

3. Do I want to spend 40 to 60 hours a week working at this position? Why or why not?

4. Do I want to spend 40 to 60 hours a week with the people I met? Why or why not?

5. From what I have been told, what parts of the job will bring me personal job satisfaction?

6. Is this position professionally challenging?

7. From what I have been told, are there any aspects of the job which don't appeal to me or I will have trouble complying with?

8. Can I work for the "new" boss?

Other questions the candidate should ask themselves are more of a personal nature, such as:

1. How does my family feel about this job or opportunity?

2. What effect will this job have on my private life?

3. Will this position ensure adequate leisure time?

4. How will it impact my outside personal interests and commitments?

5. Will this position require a move?

If there is any disparity or hesitation when considering the above questions, then consider another job position.

Character Circles

The candidate can also use Character Circles to determine if they are a good fit for the position. This method helps assess how closely their skills, abilities, interests and hobbies or personal characteristics match the requirements needed to perform the job.

First, the candidate lists all of their attributes, competencies and interest along with the job competencies and requirements in circles like those below:

THE THREE CIRCLES OF EMPLOYMENT CHARACTER

Next, determine which of those attributes, competencies and interest agree with those needed in the position. This area of mutual interest is called *character compliance*. The more attributes, competencies and interest which match the job requirements, the greater the *character compliance* will be.

The candidate should be honest and realistic during this process. They may be able to produce excellent visual aids from an Excel spreadsheet but if they prefer working with people versus a computer, this is not a skill listed in the *character compliance area*. Only those skills and abilities of interest should be placed in the *character compliance*. The more the candidate's skills, abilities and interest match the functions of the position, the greater their personal job satisfaction will be.

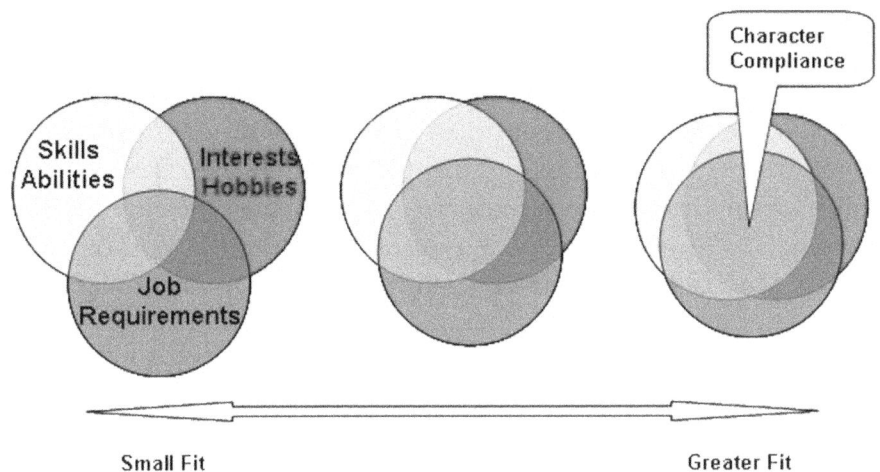

HOW WELL DOES YOUR CHARACTER COMPLIANCE "FIT"
THE POSITION?

Usually in every job, there are functions or duties which are not appealing. That is part of the job. However, using the above method, the candidate compares all the job duties and determines job compatibility. The greater the compatibility, the greater the job satisfaction will be. A candidate with a low compatibility should look at other opportunities. The job decision can be based upon how closely the job matches the candidate's personal satisfaction. This will set up the candidate for success and not failure.

Background Checks

All large companies and most small to mid-size companies conduct some type of background or drug screening for applicants. There are several business reasons for these checks. Three of the major factors are: the emphasis on security and identity verification since 9/11, the increasing cost of a bad hiring decision, plus, false information provided on resumes and job applications.

An employment background report may vary from employer to employer. The more information a company requests, the more they will pay for the background check. Some employers only check for mimial information such as a social security number while others are an all-inclusive dossier containing verified information on educational degrees, certifications, former employers, court records, driving violations, credit reports, criminal checks and even references.

In order to request a specific consumer credit report, the prospective employer must notify the candidate in writing of this requirement and obtain the candidate's written permission to conduct the employment background screening for financial responsibility.

Some specific jobs for government positions are required by Federal and State laws to conduct background checks. Some companies even ask for a previous pay stub as proof of employment.

Most companies have a very standardized hiring process and their background checks are part of the standard operating procedures for new hires. This helps to insure each candidate is treated fairly and equitably.

Never lie or provide false or misleading information on an employment application or during the interview. When the company determines the information given was false, the employment process will stop immediately and the candidate will not be considered further. The candidate *may* be given the opportunity to refute the information but a very negative impression has been created and it will be hard to overcome.

*Provide accurate information
on the application and
during the interview*

Get Started

Don't delay – do at least one thing today – now.

- Create your resume
- Review your current resume
- Update your current resume
- Ask a friend to review your resume
- Review worksheets in Appendix
- Create a positive affirmation
- Create a list of potential employers
- Create a list of friends and associates to enlist in your job search
- Visit the local unemployment office
- Conduct research on companies, industries, career interests
- Visit the local library for research materials
- _____
- _____

A body in motion stays in motion.

Set your goals – daily and weekly.

Update or fine tune your goals as part of your journey.

Congratulations on getting started and best wishes in your future job!

Make It Happen!

APPENDICES

APPENDIX A

Personal Stress Plan

The following items will help me cope with stress in my life:

One item I can do every day:

One item I can do once a week:

One item I can do once a month:

One item I can change:

One item I need to accept:

APPENDIX B

Stress

At the first sign that we may be in danger, this message is transmitted to two separate areas of the brain. One area is the prefrontal cortex, located directly behind your forehead. The prefrontal cortex is involved in judgment and thinking. It integrates the past with the present and anticipates the future. It balances experience with perception to determine appropriate action. The other area is the limbic system where the hypothalamus is located. The brain activates the HPA system (Hypothalamic-Pituitary-Adrenal system) immediately upon receipt of a threat message. In cases of threat or danger, our limbic system automatically reacts versus giving our prefrontal cortex time to analyze the situation.

The hypothalamus, located deep in the brain, senses trouble and triggers the production and release of hormones (glucocortoids), including the primary stress hormone, Cortisol. Cortisol is very important in marshaling systems throughout the body (including the heart, lungs, circulation, metabolism, immune systems and skin) to deal quickly with the danger. The hormones stream from the adrenal gland, located near the kidneys, and enter the bloodstream sounding the alarm.

The HPA system also releases certain neurotransmitters (chemical messengers) called catecholamines, particularly those known as dopamine, morepinephrine, and epinephrine (also called adrenaline.)

Catecholamines activate an area inside the brain called the amygdala, an area located deep within the brain. The amygdala then alters other brain regions. This is important to note, because the amygdala is involved in remembering emotional events.

Neurotransmitters then signal the hippocampus (a nearby area in the brain) to store the emotionally loaded experience in long-term memory. In primitive times, this combination of responses would have been essential for survival, when long-lasting memories of dangerous stimuli would be critical for avoiding such threats in the future.

During a stressful event, catecholamines also suppress brain activity concerned with short-term memory, concentration, inhibition, and rational thought. This allows a person to react quickly, to either fight or take flight.

As the danger comes closer, the heart rate and blood pressure increase instantaneously.

- Breathing becomes rapid and lungs take in more oxygen.

- Blood flow may actually increase 300% to 400%, priming the muscles, lungs, and brain for added demands.

- The spleen discharges red and white blood cells, allowing the blood to transport more oxygen.

The effect on the immune system is similar to marshalling a defensive line of soldiers to potentially critical areas.

- The steroid hormones dampen parts of the immune system, so that infection fighters (including important white blood cells) or other immune molecules can be redistributed.

- These immune-boosting troops are sent to the body's front lines where injury or infection is most likely, such as the skin, the bone marrow, and the lymph nodes.

Fluids are diverted from nonessential locations, including the mouth. This causes dryness and difficulty in talking. In addition, stress can cause spasms of the throat muscles, making it difficult to swallow.

The stress effects divert blood flow away from the skin to support the heart and muscle tissues. (This also reduces blood loss in the event that the danger catches up.) The physical effect is a cool, clammy, sweaty skin. The scalp also tightens so that the hair seems to stand up.

Stress shuts down digestive activity, a nonessential body function during short-term periods of physical exertion or crisis.

Once the threat has passed and the effect has not been harmful, the stress hormones return to normal. This is known as the relaxation response. In turn, the body also returns to normal.

APPENDIX C

Stress Symptoms

Highlight or circle all that apply:

Physical

Upset stomach . . . trouble sleeping . . . accidents and injuries . . . headaches

tight chest or throat . . . backaches . . . constipation . . . loss of appetite

diarrhea . . . exhaustion . . . wanting to sleep all the time . . . gaining weight

Mental

Trouble concentrating . . . difficulty making decision . . . fear of failure

"Why me?" . . . "What did I do wrong?" . . . scary thoughts . . . forgetfulness

suicidal thoughts . . . making errors . . . repetitive thoughts . . . no motivation

Emotional

Grumpy . . . tense . . . impatient . . . hopeless . . . easily upset . . . cry easily

no pleasure in pastimes . . . lonely . . . depressed . . . wants to be left alone

Behavioral

Excessive drinking . . . excessive smoking . . . change in sleeping habits

poor eating habits . . . driving too fast . . . drug use . . . getting into arguments

want to be alone . . .criticizing others a lot . . . want to stay in the house

getting dressed to go out becomes a chore

**This information is for informational purposes only.
Please consult your family physician.**

APPENDIX D

Relaxation Techniques

Everyone should develop methods for relaxing. Relaxation lowers blood pressure, respiration and pulse rates, releases muscle tension, and eases emotional strains. A combination of techniques seems to work best. However, the response is highly individualized and can be very effective.

Deep Breathing Exercises.

During stress, breathing becomes shallow and rapid. Taking a deep breath is an automatic and effective technique for winding down. Deep breathing exercises consciously intensify this natural physiologic reaction and can be very useful during a stressful situation, or for maintaining a relaxed state during the day.

- Inhale through the nose slowly and deeply to the count of ten. (Make sure that the stomach and abdomen expand but the chest does not rise up.)

- Exhale through the nose, slowly and completely, also to the count of ten.

- To help quiet the mind, concentrate fully on breathing and counting through each cycle.

Repeat five to ten times and make a habit of doing the exercise several times each day, even when not feeling stressed.

Meditation

Meditation is now widely practiced in this country as a relaxation technique. The goal of all meditative procedures is to quiet the mind (essentially, to relax thought). Some recommend meditating for no longer than 20 minutes in the morning after awakening and then again in late afternoon before dinner. Even once a day is helpful. It can be difficult to quiet the mind, so don't be discouraged by lack of immediate results. A few of the techniques are discussed here.

Mindfulness Meditation

Mindfulness is a common practice that focuses on breathing. It employs the basic technique used in other forms of meditation.

- Sit upright with the spine straight, either cross-legged or sitting on a firm chair with both feet on the floor, uncrossed.

- With the eyes closed or gently looking a few feet ahead, observe the exhalation of the breath.

- As the mind wanders, one simply notes it as a fact and returns to the "out" breath. It may be helpful to imagine one's thoughts as clouds dissipating away.

Mini-Meditation

The method involves heightening awareness of the immediate surrounding environment. Choose a routine activity when alone. For example:

- While washing dishes concentrate on the feel of the water and dishes.
  - Allow the mind to wander to any immediate sensory experience (sounds outside the window, smells from the stove, colors in the room).
  - If the mind begins to think about the past or future, abstractions or worries, redirect it gently back.

- While walking outside concentrate on your natural surroundings.

❧ Allow the mind to wander to any immediate sensory experience (sounds of birds, smell of flowers, colors of blooms, sky, leaves).

❧ If the mind begins to wander, redirect it gently back.

This redirection of your thoughts and worries to your senses disrupts the stress response and helps promotes relaxation. It also emphasizes an emotional and sensual appreciation of simple pleasures already present in your life.

Muscle Relaxation.

Muscle relaxation techniques, often combines with deep breathing, are simple to learn and very useful for getting to sleep. In the beginning it is useful to have a friend or partner check for tension by lifting an arm and dropping it; the arm should fall freely. Practice makes the exercise much more effective and produces relaxation much more rapidly. (Maintain a slow, deep breathing pattern throughout this exercise.)

❧ Lie down in a comfortable position without crossing the limbs, concentrate on each part of the body.

❧ Tense each muscle as tightly as possible for a count of five to ten and then release it completely.

❧ Experience the muscle as totally relaxed and lead-heavy.

❧ Begin with the top of the head and progress downward to focus on all the muscles in the body.

❧ Be sure to include the forehead, ears, eyes, mouth, neck, shoulders, arms and hands, fingers, chest, belly, thighs, calves, and feet.

**This material is for informational purposes only!
Consult your family physician for any medical advice or treatment.**

APPENDIX E

Budgets

There are several ways to limit your expenses once you understand your budget. It all starts with your monthly household income and ends with the normal monthly expenses. It is really important to keep it simple and to be honest. Honesty will help keep you out of trouble and spending more than you are bringing home. Ideally you should be working to save money at this time because it will bring more breathing room during the job search.

This is where the use of credit cards is not recommended. Pay for everything with cash, debit card, or a check from a balanced check book. You will be surprised at how difficult it is to overspend and how unimportant goods or services become once you pay for them on-the-spot with finality.

Remember when goods or services are acquired with credit, the only person who is financially satisfied is the merchant. You still have not paid the bill yet, but, trust me, it will come due. When goods and services are acquired thru a credit card and the monthly statement is not paid in full, then whatever you purchased and got a great deal on continues to be more expensive. You will probably end up paying more than it was worth. Just think of it as a $20.00 cheeseburger.

Yearly expenses, such as: insurance and taxes, must be budgeted for on a monthly basis to help meet all your obligations.

For future planning purposes, any normal monthly expenses should be analyzed over a twelve month period to determine the average monthly cost. Knowing what your average monthly expenses are will help determine a salary range compatible with your spending.

Remember the further your savings go, the more time you will have to find a career.

For more information on budgeting, please visit the following websites:

www.thebeehive.org
www.fpaforfinancialplanning.org

To determine your personal monthly budget on the next page:

Add up your net income and subtract your expenses and what you have left over goes to savings. This example is very basic, but can be used to get you started. Implementing this simple spreadsheet will provide a proactive analysis of your expenses. If you find a shortfall in meeting your obligations, begin to access your expenses and get rid of those that are not important or of real value. The overall goal is a healthier, financial future.

BEST FOOT FORWARD

Sample Budget

Monthly Income (Net – after all deductions: paycheck, alimony received, child support)		
Expenses		
Household		
Rent or mortgage		
Utilities (Electricity, Gas, Water, Sewer, Telephone)	+	
Food (Groceries, restaurants)	+	
Clothes (Children, Business	+	
Maintenance (Home, car, laundry, toiletries)	+	
Transportation (Gas, license fees, parking fees, bus, cab)	+	
Debt (Car payment, credit cards, loans)	+	
Child Support or Alimony	+	
Entertainment (Cable, satellite, internet, magazines, movies, travel)	+	
Other	+	
Other	+	
Household Total (Place the total in both spaces)	=	-
Taxes (Income on self employment, property, local)		-
Insurance (Home, rental, auto, life, health)		-
Any other one time expense or debt (School, etc.)		-
Net Income (Monthly Income – Monthly Expenses)		

To download a budget form, go to
www.bestfootforwardcareer.com/budget

APPENDIX F

Positive Affirmations

Positive affirmations or statements can be helpful in creating a positive, confident and assured presence. Using positive affirmations create new mental patterns which in turn affects our physical and emotional well-being.

Successful affirmations employ two focusing techniques, intention and expectation, followed by action. Intention refers to a result, purpose or end. It is what we "want to be." Expectation deals with believing we have achieved our intention. The key to using positive affirmations is to do so *with* action –the key word being *action*. Action is planned personal behavior. This action reinforces the affirmation.

Write down your affirmations, state them in the present tense, say them aloud several times a day, engage your imagination and **most importantly**, take action on the affirmation.

Using the affirmations below as an example, please create your specific affirmations for your current and future situation.

> ❧ I am calm and professional
>
> ❧ I am a successful ...
>
> ❧ I am creative or I have new ideas daily
>
> ❧ I efficiently use my time and resources
>
> ❧ I am ...
>
> ❧ _____
>
> ❧ _____
>
> ❧ _____

Once the affirmation has been created, next determine what action or actions will help reinforce the affirmation.

Affirmation:_____

Action:_____

_____

Start slowly. Actions are the key to successfully implementing affirmations.

Remember to keep it simple: Use only one affirmation at a time. Affirmations are meant to give you confidence not add another stress factor in your life. Do what works for you.

APPENDIX G

My Profile

Instructions for filling out the Profile Worksheet

Start with listing your interests. What do you like to do? What are the things you enjoyed doing at work? What would you do if money was no object? What hobbies do you pursue? Are there projects you always volunteer for?

Next, list your skills and abilities. What technical expertise do you possess or technical certifications have you earned? (Degrees, certifications, software/hardware knowledge, job specific expertise) What functional competencies have you mastered? (Organizational skills, communication skills, managerial skills, etc.) Typically, functional skills are divided into three distinct work-related areas:

1. **Data** – analytical, design, etc.

2. **People** – coordinate, mentor, etc.

3. **Things**- assemble, design, etc.

Next list your personal traits. These are adjectives which describes your personal attributes (dependable, attention to detail, organized, honest, etc.). For a more realistic viewpoint, ask those around you to describe your behavior and attitude.

BEST FOOT FORWARD

My Profile

Interests: Things I like to do, things I enjoy doing at work, hobbies, etc.

1. _____
2. _____
3. _____
4. _____
5. _____

Skills/Abilities: Technical expertise, functional competencies, etc.

1. _____
2. _____
3. _____
4. _____
5. _____

Personal Traits:

1. _____
2. _____
3. _____
4. _____
5. _____
6. _____

7. _____

8. _____

9. _____

10. _____

APPENDIX H

Job Skills

For employment purposes, there are three different skill sets employers consider when looking at candidates and the job requirements, they are:

1. **Specific abilities or content skills – Unique skills required for the particular job**
   Such as but not limited to:
   > *Degrees, certifications, diplomas*
   > *Software/technology knowledge: (Database Management, Security, MS Certifications, etc)*
   > *Specific job content: (Quality Control, Audit Procedures, Lean Manufacturing, etc)*
   > *Ability to operate specialized equipment: (Welding, Cranes, etc)*
   > *Best practices in industry/Familiarity with industry procedures: (Six Sigma, Quality Circles, etc)*

2. **Functional or transferable skills – General skills**
   Some examples of general business skills:
   > Time management
   > Communication
   > Organizational
   > Leadership/Supervisory

3. **Adaptive skills or self-management skills – Personal characteristics**
   Some examples of personal characteristics:
   > Self-starter
   > Dependable
   > Team player
   > Honest/Integrity
   > Detailed oriented

For each of the three skill sets above, a small sampling or example has been given. Each job/position will have its specific skill set or competencies. Knowing in advance what these skill sets are will help a candidate prepare for the interview. Asking and receiving a detailed job description **before** the interview is a plus for any candidate.

To be better prepared for an interview, create a personal written example (the Behavioral Instance detailed earlier) to provide a showcase of your characteristics using the guide on the next page: Job Skills Worksheet.

BEST FOOT FORWARD

Job Skill Worksheet

Hint: Remember you're A, B, C's

Job Skill:_____
    Assignment:

    Behavior:

    Consequence:

Job Skill:_____
    Assignment:

    Behavior:

    Consequence:

Job Skill:_____
    Assignment:

    Behavior:

    Consequence:

APPENDIX I

Personality Traits

You may also want to find a position that matches with your personality traits.   Knowing your traits will help you in this search.

Characteristics – Highlight or circle each item that describes your work habits or personal characteristics:

Neat, tidy work area . . .messy, cluttered work area . . . always busy . . . like to reflect

like to learn new things . . . maintain current work flow . . . help others

focused on doing my job . . . like fast paced work . . .like steady, even work

like supervising others . . . like non-supervisory role . . . accurate with details

more concerned with big picture . . . like working with numbers . . . imaginative

like working with people . . . completes the task . . . hold others accountable

early morning person . . . late morning person . . . easy to get along with

motivate others . . . prefer night shift . . . prefer midnight shift . . . night owl

take short cuts if possible . . . always follows every direction . . . self disciplined

resourceful . . . responsible . . . sense of humor . . . sensitive . . . practical . . . dreamer

problem-solver . . . thrifty . . . loyal . . . assertive . . . passive . . . flexible . . . delegates

industrious . . . trustworthy . . . self-confident . . . modest . . . logical . . . optimistic

open-minded . . . organized . . . deals with ambiguity . . . meet deadlines . . . quiet

team player . . . methodical . . . spontaneous . . . patient . . . eager . . . cheerful

creative thinker . . . analytical thinker . . . honest . . . compassion . . . perseverance

take initiative . . . exercise self-control . . . self-reliant . . . enthusiastic . . . courteous

somber . . . independent . . . dependable . . .like structure . . . hard worker

APPENDIX J

Strengths & Weaknesses

Once your interest, skills/abilities and character traits are determined, the next step is: knowing your strengths and weaknesses. List at least two or three strengths and weaknesses to discuss.

Strengths:

1. _____

2. _____

3. _____

Weaknesses:

1. _____

2. _____

3. _____

Be ready to talk about both in a positive manner. One or two may be weaknesses which are now strengths – relay why they were weaknesses and how each was transformed into strengths.

You may also want to relate how relying on a strength got you into trouble and what you did about it such as: Time Management – overextended yourself too much.

Review old performance reviews, talk with co-workers or current bosses if appropriate, a spouse or significant other, children also may be able to help in this area as well.

Be specific and brief in your answers.

Some companies may ask you to set up appointments (phone interviews) with former bosses – be prepared. If appropriate, discuss your new career goals with your former bosses and update them on your career search. Talk with your former bosses about performance.

APPENDIX K

Elevator Speech Examples

I have eight years experience as a sales representative. I sold water treatment systems to large shrimp farmers in the southeast region of the U.S. from south of the Ohio River to east of the Mississippi River. I also scheduled all my appointments, managed my $40,000 travel budget and schedule, and initiated sales calls with most of my customers. For the past four years, I exceeded my sales goals by at least 15% each year and stayed within the travel budget. I have recently augmented my degree in Chemistry with several Business Management classes.

I received an associate degree in drafting from the Community College. During the past three years, I have taken additional computer-programming classes. I was employed as a drafter for ABC Engineering for the past five years. Major projects I have worked on include new sewer installations, remodeling older municipal buildings and creating greenways for recreational purposes. The cost of these projects ranged from half a million to six million dollars. After four semesters of computer programming classes, I was given additional budgeting responsibility. I enjoy my work and find it rewarding to help create something from nothing.

I have twelve years experience in the retail industry. Dealing with the public on a daily basis, my psychology degree came in handy. I was the assistance floor manager of Green's where I helped manage 12 sales associates. My specific responsibilities included scheduling, training and customer service. For the past four years, my department met or exceeded the sales goal by 20% due in part, I believe, to a recognition program which I initiated and the training they received.

Elevator Speech

List three to four major strengths to include in your Elevator Speech:

1. _____
   _____
   _____

2. _____
   _____
   _____

3. _____
   _____
   _____

4. _____
   _____
   _____

Once you have created your Elevator Speech on the next page, practice it out loud.

Ask for feedback. Edit as necessary. May need to modify for different situations.

It should be comfortable and easy for you to say. Don't be embarrassed by your strong points. Women, especially, have a hard time talking about themselves. Now is the time to inform others of your unique skills and abilities in a concise and professional manner.

BEST FOOT FORWARD

Your Elevator Speech

Create an Elevator Speech incorporating the strengths listed on the previous page using a conversational tone.

Be brief; keep it 30 seconds or less. Use complete sentences. Review examples on previous page.

_____

_____

_____

_____

_____

_____

_____

_____

_____

_____

_____

_____

_____

_____

_____

_____

_____

_____

APPENDIX L

Common Interview Questions

Common questions asked during an interview and how to answer:

Tell me about yourself?

> This question provides a great opportunity to expand your 30- second summary into a two- to three-minute drill. Since the question is broad and general, it can stump the unprepared interviewee. Sometimes people think the interviewer wants to obtain personal information instead of career information. You should always answer this question as a business-related question. This two- to three-minute drill is your sales pitch.

> You should highlight the specific past work experiences that demonstrate your capabilities in the areas of the organization's needs or problems. Keep your response related to those achievements that would show you are a good candidate for the position.

> This two- to three-minute drill should be written down and practiced as you would practice giving a speech. It should not be overly rehearsed or appear to be memorized.

What did you like the most about your last job?

> As much as possible, talk about the positive aspects of the job that would be similar to the position you are interviewing for. Give examples in which you demonstrated relevant skills.

What did you like the least?

This is a little more difficult to answer. You want to avoid indicating an aspect that is prevalent in the job you are interviewing for. In addition, you don't want to complain about a previous position or company. Stay positive in your response. One strategy is to indicate a minor issue you were able to resolve or overcome. However, you may be better off being honest rather than "correct" especially if you truly dislike or want a change – example, travel. If you traveled extensively in your previous position and now want to be based near your home, it is better to inform your future employer of this decision.

What are your greatest strengths?

Be specific and honest. Give brief examples to illustrate your accomplishments. Emphasize the areas that relate to the job you are interviewing for. Don't exaggerate your accomplishments; you will appear dishonest if you do.

What are your greatest weaknesses?

Don't say that you have none. After all, few of us are perfect, and you want to be straightforward and sincere. Give examples of areas you are trying to improve. Some areas might even be seen as a strength, such as trying too hard and being a workaholic or a perfectionist.

How did you change or improve the nature of your job?

Talk about key accomplishments or areas where you identified improvements in processes or procedures. This is a chance for you to shine, but keep it brief.

What do you look for in a job?

Talk in terms of opportunities, doing quality work, being recognized, contributing, advancing, growing, and becoming a valuable part of the firm. Try to include some of the areas the interviewer previously mentioned would be a part of the new position.

Be careful when talking about advancement. Most employers like ambition, but they don't want someone who sees this job as a mere stepping-stone.

What are your long-range goals? / Where do you see yourself in 5 years or 10 years?

This tends to be a question to test your level of ambition. However, in today's economic marketplace it is difficult to predict realistic goals for the future. Mention that you would be an employee of the company, perhaps in a higher level position.

If you are interested in pursuing a higher degree or specific certifications, now is the time to mention those goals.

One strategy is to ask the interviewer, "What is the method for setting goals and when and how are they reviewed?"

What career options do you have right now?

Talk about general areas of interest rather than specific job options.

Keep it brief and concentrate on task, results, and responsibilities.

What do you think of your boss?

Regardless of what you really think of your current or previous boss or what your working relationship was, be positive. Talking negatively sheds a negative light on you as a potential candidate. (Remember, when you point a finger at someone, three are pointing back at you!)

What do you know about our company?

This is where your research about the organization will be beneficial. Give the interviewer information you obtained from your research and ask a question about something you read which will show the level of research you conducted.

Why do you want to work for us?

Talk about contributions you could make and ways in which you could become a part of their team. If it's appropriate, you could also mention the company's good reputation or position in the industry or relate how well their mission or vision statement are compatible with your goals and ideas.

What do you find most attractive about this job? Least attractive?

Mention three to four attractive features and professional reasons for their appeal.

State only one unattractive feature. (Let them know it is a minor issue.)

What are your salary expectations?

> Avoid answering this question directly with an exact monthly or annual salary figure. Instead, give a salary range which includes the minimum amount you would be willing to accept. The range gives you more negotiation power when you are later given an employment offer.

> Information on salary ranges can be found on the web at www.salary.com for most professional positions or at National College and Employers Association, www.naceweb.org for new college graduates.

APPENDIX M

Tough Interview Questions

Why were you laid off from your previous position?

> Keep your answer general and related to the business reasons for the layoff. Do not take any personal responsibility or say anything negative which could adversely impact your candidacy, especially about the company, your former boss, etc. **Do not** get emotional. Definitely practice your answer to this question *before* the interview.

What have you been doing during this period of unemployment?

> Keep your answer positive and talk about the productive aspects of your job search. If you took time off to explore other options or to go away on vacation to clear your mind, explain the results of your endeavors in results-oriented terms.

What would you do if your previous employer called you back?

> Confirm your desire to have a stable working environment and a position which is professionally rewarding.

Why would you want to consider our job since we would be paying you less than you were previously making?

> One strategy is to say you have realized pay is not as significant as you might have previously thought or since you were unemployed for a few months, you have streamlined your monthly budget and are able to live with less income.

> The best strategy is to focus on your interest in the job satisfaction and challenge this position would bring you.

Why should we hire you? / Why do you think you are a good candidate for our position?

> Discuss your skills, abilities, accomplishments, and previous work experience and how it relates to what the job requires. Use this question as an opportunity to highlight significant points or specific strengths you possess.

What can you do for us that someone else can't?

> State: *"Although I don't know the qualifications of the other candidates for the position, I think my qualifications are very strong."*

> Then repeat, at least two, of your strengths and how they relate to the open position. Concentrate on the appropriate accomplishments you feel the proudest about in answering this question. This is not the time to be humble but it is also not the time for arrogance either. Be professional, assertive and polite when answering.

How would you define success? How successful have you been?

> Answer sincerely according to your own values and needs. It helps to have a measure of success in mind. People usually focus on accomplishments, providing for family, job satisfaction, etc.

APPENDIX N

Sample Cover Letter

May 22, 2009

856 Greenleaf Circle
Pittsburgh, PA 15222

Mr. William Black
Director, Accounting
WPB Company
2000 Commerce Drive
Nashville, TN 46614

Dear Mr. Black:

I am writing in response to classified ad in XYZ Newspaper on Sunday, May 24th for an Accounting Analyst. The opportunity presented in this listing is very appealing, and I believe my experience and education will make me a competent candidate for this position.

During the past nine years, I have worked in a similar position. I utilized my analytical skills on a variety of projects which directly impacted the company's bottom line. Two examples are: implementation of computer conferencing and outsourcing of specific human resources functions. These two projects have saved the company over $1.5 million in the past year alone. Two of my other key strengths are initiative and customer service. These are vital for success in the business environment today.

I hope you'll find my experience and expertise as intriguing as I found your advertisement. Thank you for your time and consideration. I would welcome the opportunity to discuss how my skills and ideas can benefit the WPB Company.

Sincerely,

Brandon Cooper

APPENDIX O

Sample Thank You Letter

May 22, 2009

382 River Road
Henderson, KY 42420

Mr. William Black
Director, Accounting
WPB Company
2000 Commerce Drive
Nashville, TN 46614

Dear Mr. Black:

Thank you for the opportunity to interview for the analyst position. It was a very informative and interesting day with you and your company.

As I discussed in my interview, after working for a large corporation for the past nine years, I am excited about the opportunities mentioned yesterday to work with a select group of individuals dedicated to the service industry. I believe my experience will support and augment these efforts. I also believe my experience with SAP will also provide additional outlets for your services as well as support your on-going projects.

I am extremely interested in working with you and would be glad to provide any additional information you require. I look forward to hearing from you.

Thank you again for your time and consideration.

Sincerely,

Brandon Cooper

APPENDIX P

Bibliography

On Death and Dying, by Dr. Elisabeth Kübler Ross. (Macmillan, 1969, 260 pp.) This is one of the most important psychological studies of the late twentieth century. The work grew out of her famous interdisciplinary seminar on death, life, and transition.

Why Zebras Don't Get Ulcers, by Robert M. Sapolsky. (W.H.Freeman & Co., 1998 (paperback), 434 pp.) Renowned stress researcher Sapolsky summarizes research on the body's response to stress, stress-related disease, and offers suggestions for how to cope with stress.

"Stress-Coping With Everyday Problems" offers practical advice from the National Mental Health Association, www.nmha.org

The American Institute of Stress, www.stress.org

American Heart Association, www.americanheart.org

Salary information: www.salary.com, www.expertsalary.com and www.naceweb.org

Internet watchdog: www.ripoffreport.com

Occupational Outlook Handbook and *Career Guide to Industries,* Bureau of Labor Statistics, www.bls.gov

Department of Labor, Jobseeker Resources, www.doleta.gov/jobseekers/career_options.cfm

Budget Worksheet: www.bestfootforwardcareer.com

Job Seeker Newsletter: www.bestfootforwardcareer.com

Dr. Pennebaker, University of Texas - http://homepage.psy.utexas.edu/HomePage/Faculty/Pennebaker/Reprints/Spera.pdf

Dr. Allen Richarson, "The Scientific Evidence for Mind Control", www.PowerOfTheMind.com

www.ingramcontent.com/pod-product-compliance
Lightning Source LLC
Chambersburg PA
CBHW051519170526
45165CB00002B/531